BUILDING THE
COLUMBIA RIVER HIGHWAY

COLUMBIA RIVER HIGHWAY

BUILDING THE
COLUMBIA RIVER HIGHWAY
THEY SAID IT COULDN'T BE DONE

PEG WILLIS

THE
History
PRESS

Published by The History Press
Charleston, SC 29403
www.historypress.net

First published 2014
Second printing 2014
Third printing 2014

Manufactured in the United States

ISBN 978.1.62619.271.3

Library of Congress Cataloging-in-Publication Data

Willis, Peg, 1946-
Building the Columbia River Highway : they said it couldn't be done / Peg Willis.
pages cm
Includes bibliographical references and index.
ISBN 978-1-54020-931-3
1. Columbia River Highway (Or.)--History. 2. Columbia River Highway (Or.)--Design and
construction. 3. Oregon--History, Local. 4. Oregon--History. 5. Oregon--Biography. I.
Title.
HE356.O7W55 2014
388.1'22097954--dc23
2014005702

To the memory of Clarence Mershon—lifelong resident of east Multnomah County, who wrote down the stories, lest we forget—and the Friends of the Historic Columbia River Highway, whose valiant efforts have worked miracles in preserving and reconnecting the fragments of this hidden beauty.

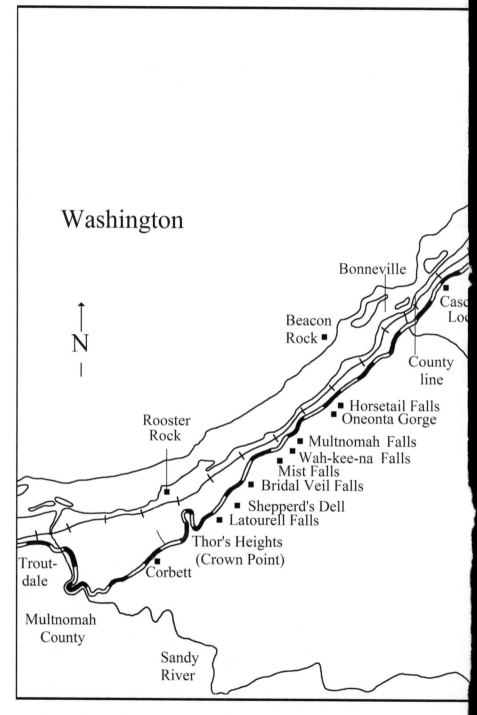

Washington

N

Bonneville

Casc
Loc

Beacon
Rock ■

County
line

Rooster
Rock

■ Horsetail Falls
■ Oneonta Gorge

■ Multnomah Falls
■ Wah-kee-na Falls
Mist Falls
■ Bridal Veil Falls

■ Shepperd's Dell
■ Latourell Falls

Thor's Heights
(Crown Point)

Trout-
dale

■
Corbett

Multnomah
County

Sandy
River

The Historic Columbia River Highway from Troutdale to The Dalles. *Map by the author.*

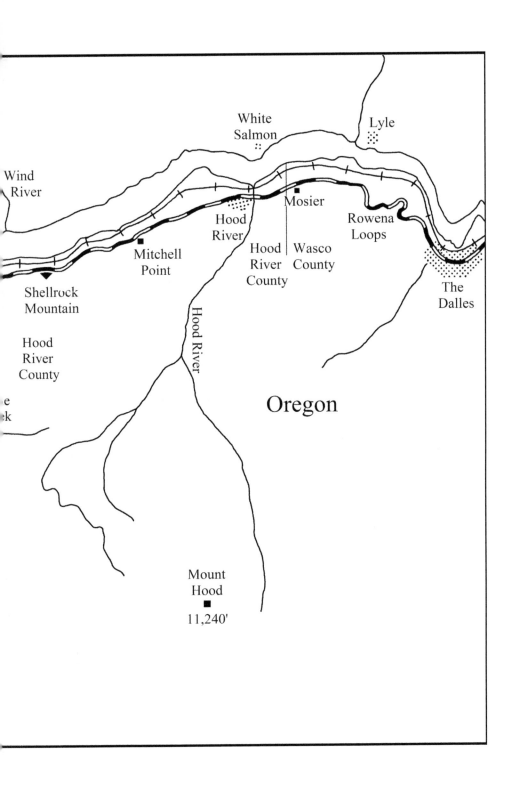

CONTENTS

CONTENTS

PREFACE

A book can never be the work of one person—especially a book such as this, which requires the assembling of many details from many sources, selected from the overwhelming abundance of information available. I would especially like to acknowledge Jeanette Kloos and David Sell. Jeanette is the former scenic area coordinator for the Oregon Department of Transportation (ODOT) and founder and president of the Friends of the Historic Columbia River Highway. David is the retired project manager with the Federal Highway Administration. Both these people have been more than generous with their many period photographs of the highway and its construction and have given generously of their time and expertise to supply answers to my questions and offer correction when I got something wrong.

Thanks also to Ellnora Lancaster Rose Young, Samuel Lancaster's great-granddaughter; Marion Ackerman Beals, daughter of Frank Ackerman, marble carver; Benny DiBenedetto, son of Gioacchino DiBenedetto, stonemason; Laura Wilt at the Oregon Department of Transportation library; Bob Hadlow, ODOT Historian, and other ODOT employees who have answered my many questions; Dave Olcott, Steve Lehl and the many other wonderful people I've met while volunteering at Vista House who have helped me fill in the story; and the many museums and historical societies that have aided my search for photos and information

Any mistakes in this book are wholly my own.

While starting with the nuts and bolts of the highway's history, for those unfamiliar with it, I have also tried to fill in the story with some of the lesser known details for the sake of those who already know and love the highway story and want to know more.

A few pronunciations:

Celilo: sə LY lo
The Dalles: the DALZ
Lancaster: **LAN** ks ter
Multnomah: mult NO mə
Oneonta: oh nee AHN tə
Oregon: OR ee gun (three syllables, not two)
Pittock: PIT ək
Spokane: spo KAN
Thor: Tor (Norwegian)
Umatilla: YOU mə **TIL** ə
Wemme: WEM ee
Willamette: wə LAM ət
Yeon: yawn

The schwa (ə) is the vowel sound in the first syllable of the word "again."

Introduction

The Gorge of the Columbia

The Columbia River is long, large, beautiful and wild. At least, it was wild in its earlier lives—of which there were several.

On its journey of 1,243 miles, it drains a total area of 259,000 square miles—roughly the size of France—from British Columbia in Canada and seven U.S. states. It serves as the border between Oregon and Washington for 300 miles and discharges 17.5 trillion gallons of water into the Pacific Ocean each year.

Several men in the history of the Pacific Northwest—men who were by nature curious and imaginative—suggested that the Columbia River watershed had been visited at sometime in the past by a massive catastrophe involving water. During the mid-1800s, Irish-born Thomas Condon (1822–1907) served as a Congregational pastor to churches in several Northwest towns—among them, The Dalles, Oregon. During his time in The Dalles, he was able to do considerable exploring in eastern Oregon and became fascinated with the landforms and fossil beds in this geologically rich area. He was especially intrigued by the presence of fossilized seashells in this arid, near-desert land.

In the next generation, Samuel Lancaster (1865–1941), designer of the Columbia River Highway, wondered whether the Columbia River Gorge had been formed by a "wall of water."[1] His suggestion came both from his knowledge of Condon's explorations and research and also from personal experience in the Gorge.

J. Harlan Bretz (1882–1981) is given credit for first speculating, and then insisting, that the scablands of eastern Washington were carved by a flood of biblical proportions. He noted the "bathtub ring" effect on the hills and felt that these massive horizontal markings could only have been produced by water washing back and forth at that level for an extended period of time. He pointed out the dry waterfalls, hanging valleys, potholes, channeled scablands, massive gravel deposits and "erratics" (isolated rocks from a foreign origin) scattered throughout the Columbia and Willamette River Valleys as further proof of his theory. And where would this unthinkably immense volume of water have come from? Some place north, Bretz speculated, and he referred to this as-yet-undiscovered source as the "Spokane Flood."

Bretz was ridiculed for his ideas. Invited in 1927 to present his findings on "The Channeled Scablands and the Spokane Flood" at the Geological Society of Washington, D.C., Bretz attended in good faith but found that the event might better have been described as an ambush.[2] He presented his information; then, one by one, his peers tore apart his beliefs. These learned men based their objections on academic knowledge rather than actual field experience in the scablands of eastern Washington. To be sure, this is the purpose of such conferences—to consider possibilities and then try to disprove them. Those ideas that cannot be disproved must be considered as possibly viable truths. But feelings were strong in opposition to Bretz's claims—very strong.

This was at a time when James Hutton's theory of uniformitarianism was holding sway.[3] Hutton's theory that "the present is the key to the past" put forth the idea that outside the occasional localized earthquake, flood or volcanic eruption, the earth continued as it had in the past and would, therefore, have taken eons to evolve to its present design. Not only that, but this extended time frame was necessary to fit in with Darwin's theory of evolution, which was gaining wider and wider support. And of course, there was no allowance for a flood anywhere near the size needed for Bretz's theory.

Uniformitarianism was in; catastrophism was out—relegated to the position of not-so-bright little sister.

The advent of flying brought much-needed support for Bretz's theory as the evidence he had gleaned so laboriously on foot became easily visible from the air. Though Bretz continued his field research for the next thirty years, he never reached the point of actually identifying the source of the massive flood(s). But his persistence—and excellent scientific practices—began to turn the tide, and in 1979, in J. Harlan Bretz's ninety-seventh year, the Geological Society of America awarded him the coveted Penrose Medal, presented to those who advance the study of the geosciences.

The first "highway" through the Columbia River Gorge was the Columbia River. *Photo by Edward S. Curtis, courtesy of Old Oregon.*

Today, Bretz's ideas have gained acceptance. The source of the massive floods been identified as glacial Lake Missoula in Montana—a lake that appears to have extended hundreds of miles east from the Idaho border. It is thought that this body of water—about half the size of Lake Michigan—was held in place by a two-thousand-foot-high ice dam, which, in times of global warming, would gradually melt and then float free, allowing the water to rush toward the sea. Geologists believe this may have happened up to forty times. An amazing thing to consider, and even more so when we realize that this immense lake would empty in as little as two weeks.

The early land highways through the Columbia River Gorge were nothing more than rabbit trails, as well as the trails of squirrels, possums, deer and bear. Animals, like water, seek the path of least resistance, but in the case of the animals, this does not necessarily mean the lowest elevation. They sought food, shelter and a place to safely breed and raise their young. And many of them migrated with the seasons.

The Native Americans, many of whom were also seminomadic, followed these trails, leaving little more trace on the land than the animals before them. Time was usually not a determining factor in selecting routes of travel. Instead, the travel itself was allowed to determine a framework for life. Eventually, the trails became wider and more established. When the white men came, seeking furs, land or gold, they quite naturally followed these age-old trails.

To the Oregon pioneers, however, time was a big factor. They needed to get to the Willamette Valley before winter set in.

The first person who tried to bring a wheeled vehicle west was Marcus Whitman—missionary to the Walla Walla, Cayuse, Umatilla and Nez Perce Indians at a place called Waiilatpu (near present-day Walla Walla, Washington). On his first trip west, he was forced to abandon his wagon before reaching his destination, but on a later trip, he helped guide the pioneers of 1843—the first big wave of settlers traveling the Oregon Trail—to Waiilatpu and beyond with their wagons.

There were dangers along the way. Every wagon train experienced tragedy in one form or another—accidents, shootings, death by disease and, in later years, trouble from Native Americans, justifiably angry about the whites taking the land they felt was theirs.

In spite of these difficulties, one of the most frightening parts of the trip was the last one hundred miles. Exhausted, after making their way overland roughly two thousand miles, intrepid travelers were faced at The Dalles (a French word meaning "cobble stones," which accurately described the riverbed at this point) with a monumental combined threat of water and mountains. As the Columbia River plunged into the great Gorge it had carved through the Cascade Mountains, land wide enough for wagons to travel alongside the river disappeared. The Columbia River was a wild and unforgiving host to these newcomers, and some died in the attempt to pass—so close to the end of their journey.

Wheels were removed from wagons, and the wagons were then placed on rafts constructed of logs. Then the pioneers boarded the rafts, knowing they were taking their lives in their hands. Animals were driven along the narrow edge of the river and would hopefully meet their owners once the rapids were passed—about forty miles below. Famous Oregon pioneer Jesse Applegate and his brother each lost a son on this stretch of river.

In 1845, only two years after the Emigrant Road began bringing people to Oregon, Samuel K. Barlow stepped forward to make a change. Barlow, unwilling to make the trip down the Columbia, teamed up with Joel Palmer, fellow traveler, and they managed to beat their way around the south shoulder of Mount Hood to arrive in Oregon City in the fall of that year. The following spring, Barlow joined with Philip Foster to create a road for wagons around the south side of the mountain, thus bypassing the treacherous stretch of river. They called it the Mount Hood Toll Road. It sounded good; many immigrants arriving in The Dalles chose to take this route, deciding that dangers unseen couldn't possibly be as frightening as those they could see all too well.

But they were mistaken. The Barlow Road, as it came to be called, was treacherous at best—especially the stretch called Laurel Hill—and more than one wagon was smashed to bits as it attempted to travel this "road."

The first Oregon pioneers settled on the west side of the Cascade Mountains. They could have avoided the dreadful travel through the Gorge by staying on the east side, but tales of Oregon's bounty all centered on the west—the Willamette Valley. Stories of amazingly fertile farmland, beautiful and bountiful crops and moderate weather had filtered back home in the few letters that gradually became a flood of correspondence. People in the eastern states began to catch that new disease—Oregon fever. And it all centered on the Oregon west of the Cascades. At this time, Oregon was not a state and had no man-made boundaries. The natural boundaries were the ocean, the Columbia River and the Cascade Mountains.

By the time the second generation was reaching maturity, people began to remember the land east of the mountains—land that had been thought of as only an "Indian infested wilderness," an obstacle to be overcome on the way to the real Oregon. They remembered the richness of the land, the beautiful prairies, the bunch grass so tall horses' bellies would vanish in it and the great wealth of natural resources. And it didn't rain all the time in Eastern Oregon!

Men came with their range animals and found the area to their liking. In time, however, they became mighty sick and tired of their own company. Wives came and then, of course, children. And with the women and children came schools and churches. The men allowed themselves to be civilized—to a certain degree.

But they were isolated. They could grow wheat—but getting it to the west side was a problem, and importing things like lemons, pineapples, pianos and printing presses was very difficult.

Stern-wheeled (or side-wheeled) steamships began plying the river in the 1850s, and the first Oregon railroad, the six-mile-long portage line near what is now the town of Cascade Locks, opened in 1855. The car, on wooden tracks, carried both goods and people and was drawn by a mule.

The next year, the first constructed wagon road opened in the Columbia River Gorge. The February 9, 1856 *Oregonian* reported, "We are informed that a new road around the portage of the Cascades, on the Oregon side, has been completed and that goods are now being transported over this road with safety and dispatch." Mr. Kilborn, the road's owner, was quoted as saying, "The road is now in complete order and my teams will always be in readiness."[4] Kilborn's road climbed from river level up over a point of rock 425 feet above the shore line and back down again. In addition to being steep, the road was bumpy and often muddy. But it was a step forward.

By the 1870s, the need for a wagon road in the Gorge was addressed by the Oregon legislature. It appropriated $50,000 for the construction of a road from Troutdale to The Dalles. When funds were exhausted in 1876, another $50,000 was dedicated to the road's completion. The resulting narrow dirt road was crooked and steep—often requiring double teams.

In 1882, the Oregon Railway & Navigation line running from Cascade Locks to Portland was constructed. The railroad ran just beside the river and a few feet above it. In the process of the railroad's construction, the road of 1876 was largely destroyed.

It wasn't that no one cared enough to construct a highway through the Gorge. Such a thing was just considered wishful thinking. James Allen, later

Keith Ticknor demonstrates high-wheeler bicycle technique. *Courtesy of Friends of the Historic Columbia River Highway.*

to be highway commissioner in Washington State, said, "You can't survey a road along the Columbia River, let alone build one."[5]

The League of American Wheelmen, organized by a new and exciting breed of Americans—men who rode bicycles for recreation—took root in 1880. It was these bicycle riders, not the automobile owners, who set the stage for the good roads movement in this country. In the late 1800s, the league began publishing a monthly magazine, *Good Roads*, which kept its members apprised of progress in the movement as well as encouraging scientific research on road construction.

With the advent of automobiles (and motorized trucks for hauling goods), the stage was set for someone to build a road through the Columbia River Gorge. Here is the story of how it happened.

PART 1

THE PEOPLE

1
SAM HILL

LARGER THAN LIFE

S am Hill was born in a small settlement called Deep River along the
Uwharrie River in North Carolina, the fourth of six children. His
mother, Eliza Mendenhall Hill, was a descendant of William Penn's
Quakers in Pennsylvania. His father, Nathan Bronson Hill, was a country
doctor. The family was highly committed to their Quaker beliefs. According
to Sam,[6] his father built the first cotton factory south of the Mason-Dixon
line, was vice-president of the Bank of North Carolina and was head of the
Underground Railroad for the state of North Carolina. Sam also reported
that his father was an advocate for the construction of better roads. As a
Quaker, Nathan was a conscientious objector and, because of this, often
found himself in "awkward" circumstances. But, said Sam, "Quakers are
accustomed to persecution, and the more they are persecuted the stronger
are their convictions and the more loyal they are to them."[7]

This attitude seems to have been exemplified in Sam's life—at least
in some areas. He was a man of strong opinions and powerful ideas, not
thwarted by difficulties or setbacks. When Hill had "a bee in his bonnet,"
things were bound to happen.

Sam tells that when he was four and a half, he and his family left the
South—by a circuitous route to avoid suspicion—and ended up in
Minneapolis, Minnesota, in September 1861.[8] One of the things young
Sam remembered from the experience was the arduous twenty-mile trip by
stagecoach from St. Paul to Minneapolis. Even at this early age, he seems to
have been impressed by the need for good roads.

Sam Hill's winning personality is evident in this photo. *Courtesy of Maryhill Museum of Art.*

After graduation from high school, Sam worked on a railroad survey crew until beginning his higher education at Haverford College. After three years at Haverford, he transferred to Harvard, where he graduated in the middle of his class. In 1880, he was admitted to the Minnesota bar and, in 1881, returned to Harvard to attend law school for a short time. This was also the year he first traveled to Europe.

Sam worked in a law office in Minneapolis for eight years. He boarded with a family who spoke only German at home, giving him the opportunity to become comfortable with this language, which he would use often in his European travels.

Sam was learning to use his assets to get ahead in the world. He subscribed to and read (when the occasion called for it) hometown newspapers from all over the state of Minnesota, traveled to small towns regularly to meet and visit with the townspeople and tried never to forget a face or name. He moved up the ladder in the law firm, started a law business of his own, began making a considerable amount of money by speculating in real estate and, in 1886, went to work for James J. Hill (no relation) in the legal department of his fast-growing Great Northern Railway. In 1888—the same year he became president of the Minneapolis Trust Company—he married the boss's daughter, Mary Frances.

In 1889, Sam and Mary Frances's daughter, Mary Mendenhall Hill, was born. She was followed in 1893 by a son, James Nathan B. Hill.

To all appearances, things were going quite well for Sam Hill. But as is often the case, the truth went deeper than appearances. His wife didn't like him. She bore him two children and lived with him for the first few years of their marriage. But this seems to have been about the extent of their relationship. Sam continued to support her and the children financially, but their contact was minimal.

Sam enjoyed his friendships with various royal families of European countries he had visited. Perhaps he felt that these relationships were appropriate for one of his station in life. In 1893, Sam met the future queen of Rumania (the common spelling at the time) Marie. He also numbered among his personal friends Leopold and Albert of Belgium; Loie Fuller, a dancer of somewhat questionable ability; and Alma Spreckles, wealthy San Francisco matron who was much enamored of Sam Hill's often bizarre plans—and perhaps Mr. Hill himself.

The Minneapolis Trust Company bought control of the Seattle Gas and Electric Company in 1895, and Sam was made president. This was Sam's first foray into the Northwest.

From Seattle, he traveled to Japan in 1897—the first of many trips to "the Orient." His varied trips were sometimes on behalf of the Great Northern Railroad and sometimes for other purposes. Perhaps in Sam's mind, these journeys opened up a bigger world to him—and it took a big world to entertain such a "big" and busy man.

In 1899, Sam Hill became the first president of the newly formed Washington State Good Roads Association. In this important area of development, Washington was way out in front of its neighbor to the south.

By 1900, Sam's interest in the railroad business was waning, possibly with some encouragement from his father-in-law, and he resigned from his railroad posts. For several years, Sam was president or director of a number of businesses, including the Seattle Gas and Electric Company and various component railroads of the Great Northern. He gradually increased his interest in real estate and stock market speculation, and he became more and more agitated about the need for good roads in America—in Washington State in particular. He talked to anyone who would listen, including the U.S. Senate Committee, which had been formed to address the subject of good roads.

In 1901, Hill's wife and children joined him for a time in Seattle. Hoping to keep them there, Sam decided to build a house and bought land for this purpose in 1902. Unfortunately, the promise of a house wasn't enough to do the job. Mary and the two children left again for the East in 1903. By this time, Sam was more actively trading in the stock market. His business savvy, with perhaps a bit of luck, was the basis of his continuing financial success. In 1904, Sam sold the Seattle gas business and began advocating with the legislature for good road laws for Washington State.

In 1905, he bought an estate in Massachusetts and a ranch in central Washington. The estate was intended as a summer home for the family—a sort of neutral ground where they could keep up the appearance of a loving marriage. Sam, however, was not impressed with Massachusetts. The estate was sold in 1913, and with it vanished any hope of maintaining appearances.

One good thing did come from the venture. Sam invited twenty of the best Italian stonemasons working on the estate to come west and apply their skills to road building. He promised to pay their current wage and board them as well, in effect increasing their pay. They accepted and became a part of the Columbia River Highway story.

The ranch was a place where Hill hoped he could bond with his son, James. Unfortunately, James was not interested in bonding with his father—at least not on Dad's terms. James was a poor student and was not interested in the kind of life his father lived. He had no desire to excel in any area of his life. This may have been partly the result of his family situation. His mother was more than just strong willed. Judging from some of Sam's correspondence, she may have had mental problems as well. Mary Mendenhall, Sam's firstborn, was sickly and apparently suffered from schizophrenia. In short, the family was never a family.

This must have weighed heavily on Sam—especially the disappointment in his son, the one he hoped would carry on his name and reputation. But it was not to be. Neither James nor Mary Mendenhall ever married. And neither became "successful" adults that Sam could be proud of.

Sam Hill was not used to having his desires go unfulfilled. He had the money, personality and social status to make things happen. But he had no heir. Perhaps hoping to remedy this lack, he entertained a series of mistresses over the years, at least three of whom bore him children.

The house Hill intended to build in Seattle was not begun until 1909—seven years after he had purchased the land with the supposed intent of building a home for his family.

In 1907, he bought seven thousand acres on the north shore of the Columbia River and began taking over a town (Columbus) that was already there. Over the next few years, he gradually expanded his plans for this farming community. He changed its name to Maryhill—in honor of his daughter, not his wife—and tried to change everything else about it as well. He began building a great mansion on the bluff overlooking the river, but it stood silent and unfinished for many years.

Sam Hill's life was a study in contrasts, both amazing and heart wrenching. But a project on the horizon—one Sam worked and longed for—was quietly gaining steam. The turning point was probably in 1906, when he met Sam Lancaster.

SAMUEL LANCASTER

HEART, SOUL AND ENGINEER

I f ever there lived a man who should have been a failure, it would be Samuel Christopher Lancaster. Born to his father's third wife (the first two died—probably in childbirth), Samuel was the sixth child in the family and was followed by three more children, born at the prescribed two-year interval. Some records give his year of birth as 1864, but Lancaster always said it was 1865.[9] Sam's father was a cotton merchant in the South, necessitating occasional moves between Pike County, Mississippi, and Jackson, Tennessee. Samuel was born in the tiny town of Magnolia, Mississippi, but spent most of his youth in Jackson.

After graduating from high school, Sam attended Southwestern Baptist University (now Union University), where he studied engineering. At the end of his first year, with funds running low, he enrolled in the school of real life experience and went to work for the Illinois Central Railroad. It is perhaps surprising to find extreme engineering skill and a reverence for beauty and the God who created it in the same man, but Samuel Lancaster was most definitely that man. Sent to work in the Yazoo Delta region in west Mississippi, Lancaster continued to refine and build on his engineering skills. It was here—where the famed Casey Jones was later to meet his fate—that Sam Lancaster nearly lost his life.

While working on a railroad grade, he and several co-workers became deathly ill after ingesting contaminated water. Two of the men died that night. Sam and one other man were shipped home to—hopefully—recover.

And recover he did. At least he recovered from the typhoid fever[10] that had laid him low. But just as the doctor was about to pronounce him well, Sam was attacked by another fearsome disease—infantile paralysis.

Known today as polio, this disease had no known cure and was every bit as much a death sentence as typhoid. As the illness swept over his body, Sam gradually lost the use of his limbs. The doctor said there was no hope of recovering the loss of function and poked needles under Sam's nails to prove the nerves were dead.

Samuel Lancaster in 1908. *Courtesy of Ellnora Lancaster Rose Young, Samuel Lancaster's great-granddaughter.*

But the nerves were not dead—Sam howled in pain, and the doctor quickly retreated. Unfortunately, neither the doctor nor anyone else had the slightest idea how to help Sam recover the use of his body. No one, that is, except Sam himself.[11]

And it had to be accomplished before things got any worse. Although Sam could still move his head and neck, his arms, legs, fingers and toes gradually were drawing up into a clawlike shape and becoming rigid, making a possible recovery only that much harder.

Sam brought his dilemma to the God he had come to love in his early years. He felt strongly that his love of beauty and engineering prowess were gifts. So if God wanted him to use these gifts, he would need to provide healing power. Young Sam Lancaster determined to try with every ounce of his strength and leave the result in God's hands.

While Sam was unable to hold reading material for himself, one day, his mother read him a story from *St. Nicholas* magazine about a boy who, though paralyzed, could draw beautiful pictures by means of a pencil clutched between his teeth.

After a bit of thinking, Sam described in detail an easel he would like constructed to sit over his chest on the bed. Then, by great effort, he was able to throw his head forward and, with a pencil clutched in his teeth, make marks on a piece of paper. Soon, he was able to write and even create clean and accurate mechanical drawings.

Next, he decided to put all his effort into moving the middle finger of one hand. Through enormous effort, he finally succeeded. This gave him hope that he might eventually recover.

He drew a design for a frame to hold him in an upright position. It was constructed for him, but when he was lifted and strapped in place, he promptly fainted. He had lain so long in a prone position his heart was not equipped to pump blood to his brain when he was upright. The scheme was given up—but only for the day. Sam tried again the next day, and the next.

One day, he slipped from the frame's constraints and fell to the floor, breaking loose his toes from the rigid position they had assumed. Though the fall was extremely painful, he found that it had put great pressure on his crippled toes forcing them to straighten. From that moment, he pushed himself mercilessly, knowing recovery was possible.

Sam realized he would need to force all his tendons to stretch back into their natural position—a very painful prospect. He had himself moved to a small cabin at the back of the property—out of hearing of those in the main house—with only one man to attend him and instructed this man to force the rigid limbs to loosen, no matter how much he might cry out in pain. He did not want his mother or sister to suffer from hearing his cries.

In time, his joints were freed, and he began the monumental task of learning to use his body again. He learned to write with a pencil stuck in a potato that he clutched in his hand,[12] eventually progressing to holding the pencil with his fingers. Even before he had completely recovered, a Jackson city official came to him with a situation that was causing difficulty for city workers. Lancaster pinpointed the problem, drew up the remedy and began to think of getting back into engineering. One of his drawings, which was displayed in a store window downtown, drew the attention of the chief engineer of one of the large railroads. He asked that the man responsible for the drawing come see him about taking charge of the railroad's masonry construction. When Lancaster arrived for the interview—still using crutches—he was greeted by a skeptical official. Obviously, this man on crutches would not be able to do the job. But when Sam, with quiet confidence, insisted he could do it, he was given a chance to prove it.[13] And he did. Before long, he began to work for the City of Jackson, and his work was so obviously superior that he was made the Madison County engineer. In a flurry of creativity, he designed and built light and water systems. He supervised the installation of sewers, hard surfaced roads, parks and other municipal projects. He also married his sweetheart, Ella Potts.

The work Lancaster did for the City of Jackson and Madison County was nothing short of astounding. He did things that had not even been thought of in other cities. And he kept careful records of money spent, man-hours required and the outcome of the work. He was only twenty-five years old at this time.

His outstanding work on the half-million-dollar road system that he created in the 1890s came to the attention of James Wilson, national secretary of agriculture. Wilson called Lancaster to Washington to discuss the need for good roads across America. Agriculture was useless to those in the cities if the farmers could not easily get their goods to market.

Realizing that in Lancaster, he had not only an outstanding engineer but also a man who could teach and persuade, Wilson invited Sam to make presentations to the legislature and, not long after that, named him consulting engineer with the Bureau of Public Roads. In 1904, Wilson sent Lancaster on a nationwide tour to "preach the gospel of good roads" to all the states in the Union (then numbering forty-three). He traveled throughout the country, preaching his message and sharing information on why and how good roads should be constructed, and returned to Jackson as often as possible, where he was still covering the post of city engineer.

The next year, the proud citizens of Jackson renamed the city park that Lancaster had designed in honor of their hometown boy who was becoming so renowned. Lancaster Park included an electro-chalybeate well,[14] a small lake with rental rowboats and canoes and walking paths in an idyllic setting—just the sort of thing Lancaster loved.

After Lancaster had visited and preached his gospel of good roads in the eastern states, he headed west to California. He met with road enthusiasts in Los Angeles County in 1906, where he received instruction, via telegram, from Secretary Wilson to proceed to Yakima, Washington, to meet with Sam Hill.

Hill, who had been serving on the Washington State Highway Board since the year before, invited Lancaster to come to Seattle with his message and knowledge. He desperately wanted this fine young engineer to come work with him. And Hill had a way of getting what he wanted—at least most of the time. He invited Lancaster to bring his family to Seattle and work in that great city for six months—all at Hill's expense. Wilson agreed to give Lancaster a six-month leave. When the six months were up, Lancaster resigned his national position and began working with Reginald H. Thompson, Seattle Parks Department commissioner, to design a $7 million system of boulevards and parks in Seattle. The Alaska-Yukon-Pacific Exhibition was planned for 1909, and Seattle wanted to shine for the event.

Lancaster Park in Jackson, Tennessee. *Author's collection.*

In the early part of 1907, Hill addressed the Washington State legislature, bringing along as his key witness, engineer Samuel Lancaster. Hill proposed several measures, all of which duly passed into law, and Washington State suddenly had the best road laws in the nation.

Hill had managed to get his friend Lancaster appointed to a full professorship and as chairman of the Highway Engineering Department—the first in the nation—at the University of Washington. Though Lancaster had taken but one year of college-level engineering, he was indisputably the national expert on the subject.

During this time, Hill continued working closely with the Washington State legislature, lobbying for good roads, especially an east–west route through the Gorge of the Columbia on the north (Washington) side of the great river.

In October 1908, Lancaster attended the First International Road Congress in Paris with Sam Hill, Reginald H. Thompson and Henry Bowlby. At the end of the very inspiring conference, Hill took his friends on an extended auto tour of several European countries, where they viewed castles on the Rhine, terraced vineyards in Italy, rock retaining walls built at the time of Charlemagne, Roman roads still functioning quite well after two thousand years and a lovely windowed tunnel on Lake Uri (an arm of Lake Lucerne) in Switzerland. Lancaster was deeply moved by the beauty and engineering perfection he viewed. When Hill insisted that such things would someday be seen in America's Pacific Northwest, his guests were impressed—and doubtful. But the seed had been sown.

3
HENRY PITTOCK

THE PORTLAND OREGONIAN

H enry Pittock was born in England in 1835. He spent his youth in Pittsburgh, Pennsylvania, after his father moved the family to America when Henry was four years old. Henry apprenticed in his father's print shop, and at the age of seventeen, he left home with a brother, Robert, to answer the siren call of the West. The two intrepid adventurers arrived in Oregon without money to support themselves and, according to some reports, without shoes as well. The year they traveled—1853—was one of the worst for disease on the trail. Many were felled by dysentery or typhoid, but the Pittock brothers survived.

Arriving in Oregon City in October, Henry first applied to the *Oregon Spectator*, the largest newspaper in the territory, but found it did not need his services. After several other disappointments, he finally went to work as a typesetter for the insignificant weekly *Oregonian* in Portland. Thomas Dryer, Pittock's boss, paid him by providing room and board. "Room" meant a space on the print shop floor where he could throw out his blankets at night, and "board" was meager. But it was enough—at least as a start.

After six months of satisfactory work, Henry was to receive an annual salary, but he never actually did. Since Dryer was more interested in politics than in running a paper, and since his business practices were not highly effective, Henry was often paid in partnership shares rather than actual salary. He gradually assumed the responsibility of manager and editor.

But Henry Pittock, an avid outdoorsman, apparently needed even more stimulation than the paper could offer him. In July 1857, he became the first recorded person to climb to the summit of Mount Hood—Oregon's highest mountain at 11,250 feet.

At the conclusion of his successful run for president, Abraham Lincoln appointed Dryer to a political position—perhaps to thank him for his editorial support during the campaign. At any rate, Dryer "gave" the much-indebted *Oregonian* to Pittock as partial payment of the salary owed, providing, of course, that Pittock was willing to take on the debt.

At this time, three other daily papers in Portland provided fierce competition. As two of these papers seemed to have a more promising outlook than the *Oregonian*, Pittock knew he needed to come up with a powerful plan if he intended to survive. On February 4, 1861, by which time seven Southern states had already seceded and a month before Lincoln took office, Pittock went daily, using a brand-new steam-powered press. The timing was perfect.

He set up a complex arrangement for getting fresh, up-to-the-minute news of the Civil War, by way of Pony Express, from the nearest existing telegraph lines in Yreka, California. His competitors, by contrast, relied on information being brought by steamer from San Francisco. News arrived at the office of the *Oregonian* days ahead of the competitions' papers.

Producing a good paper was one thing, but keeping it solvent was something else. Pittock began requiring cash payments for subscriptions—a task made easier as patrons realized the superiority of the *Oregonian*. He also sought to collect from accounts left delinquent by Dryer. With this new financial security, he invested heavily in new equipment, choosing to have the very best in his attempt to stay ahead of the competition.

As Pittock was gradually able to look beyond the paper for investment opportunities, he bought shares in a couple paper mills, which, incidentally, provided newsprint for his papers (yes, papers—plural. He established the *Portland Evening Telegram*, a second newspaper, in 1877.) In 1884, he again bought updated presses, raising the printing speed to twenty-four thousand copies per hour.

As time went on, Pittock began investing in banks, real estate, transportation and the lumber business. He and his family—his wife, Georgiana, and their five children—lived in a very small, insignificant house during these years, as Pittock invested his earnings in other ways.

As the first decade of the twentieth century drew to a close, Henry Pittock, formerly a penniless, barefoot immigrant, was in a position to support future growth and progress in any way he chose. He had money and influence and used both liberally in the projects that appealed to him. Fortunately, a highway through the Gorge of the Columbia was on his list of interests.

4
SAM JACKSON

THE JOURNAL MAN

Born on September 15, 1860, in Deltaville, Virginia, C.S. (Samuel) Jackson grew into a young man with a flair for business. At age sixteen, he spent fifteen dollars his father had given him on a small printing press he happened to find. He used his new purchase to print business cards and letterheads—the beginning of a useful career in the field of printing.

Hearing encouraging stories from friends of the family who had settled in the West, Sam decided, at age twenty, to give it a try. He took a train to San Francisco, then a ship to Portland. He traveled up the Columbia River by boat as far as Umatilla Landing and then took the stage to the little town of Pendleton, where his friends had settled, arriving in the spring of 1880.

He worked at first for the Utah, Idaho and Oregon Stage Company and was soon named agent. When writing to his father about this, he mentioned that he was paid forty dollars a month. His father responded (according to Sam), "Don't take the money; you aren't worth it."[15] It may have happened that way, or it may have been just an interesting tale Sam liked to tell on himself. Like all good newsmen, he had a flair for making a story interesting. He also said that he got the job as agent because "a man homelier than Abe Lincoln was bound to be reliable."[16]

Jackson joined the publishing team at the *East Oregonian* on August 3, 1881, at age twenty, and with a partner, J.A. Guyer, bought out the paper for $3,500 in January 1882.

Before Jackson, the newspaper had been typical of a young, raw western town. The reporting was slanted, and the editorials were shamelessly ignorant, prejudiced and sometimes downright hateful. Sam Jackson changed all that. His take on the newspaper business was "print the truth. Fight for the right. People like a fighting newspaper."[17]

Jackson was a young man of integrity, and he expected others to measure up to that same standard. He was neither afraid of hard work nor ashamed to save a penny. His editorials called others to those high principles. He was a Democrat and insisted that the paper would always remain a voice for the Democratic Party. He took the side of the poor and downtrodden against the rich and powerful.

Jackson kept his finger on the pulse of the community in a number of ways. In addition to his work on the *EO*, he became a representative of a book publishing firm, opened a general insurance agency combined with the sale of real estate and started a bicycle agency. But the paper was his first love.

He had a great sense of humor coupled with a quick wit and strong opinions. At one point, after changing the masthead of the paper, he wrote, "We respectfully invite the criticism of the press, and the man that writes something that does not suit us, we will send him our mother-in-law's picture in a frame."[18] Fortunately, Sam was not yet married.

The newspaper under Sam Jackson's leadership was not afraid to take on unpopular causes. Sam felt that the misuse of alcohol was a detriment to society. He thought gossip was the pastime of the ignorant, extending credit was unwise, dishonest people weren't born but made and violence and gambling needed to be stopped. And he said so.

He took particular care to warn mothers not to let their daughters go out in the evening, supposedly to visit a friend, if they were actually "gadding around the street waving handkerchiefs at men with or without reputation." Anxious not to be misunderstood on this important point, he added, "Flirtation of any kind, particularly when carried on in the street is on the road to ruin, which surely leads to ill fame and then to hell as fast as women and wine can travel together."[19]

The 1880s were years of growth in Umatilla County, as elsewhere in the state, and the newspaper needed to grow with the population. Jackson went to San Francisco and purchased steam fittings to power a new, larger press.

Not long after Jackson took over the *East Oregonian*, J.P. Wager entered the picture and was soon in the position of editor, while Jackson focused on the business end of the operation. Wager and Jackson were both men of strong opinion. But for the most part, they agreed on controversial subjects, and the partnership was a good one. Wager was elected to the Oregon State

Senate in 1887 but continued his duties at the *EO* until 1890, when he rather abruptly moved to Portland.

Even at his young age, Sam Jackson was well respected in the newspaper business. A rival newspaper, the *Athena Republican*, wrote, "Although a great many express a great dislike for Editor Jackson it must be admitted that the *East Oregonian* is the best newspaper in the county for news."[20]

The *Walla Walla Town Talk* spoke of him as "by the way, the best 'newspaper rustler' east of the mountains; and who is making the *E.O.* a credit not only to the section it represents but to journalism throughout the state."[21]

Jackson's marriage in 1886 to Maria Clopton seems not to have changed his newspaper habits in any way—although, hopefully, he ceased printed references to his mother-in-law. He continued promoting the same values and projects as in his former days.

On more than one occasion during his Pendleton days, Jackson's "enthusiasm" got him into trouble. He was twice reported as being involved in fisticuffs over comments made about the *East Oregonian*. Here is one report:

> *The two men met on the street and Hendricks called Jackson a liar. Jackson slapped his face. Hendricks hit Jackson with his cane which the* E.O. *account described as loaded, and while Hendricks also was applying epithets to Jackson, Marshal Means chanced by. He arrested Hendricks for using profane and abusive language on the streets. Hendricks was fined twenty dollars.*[22]

Progress was a good thing in Sam Jackson's mind. And he was prophetic in his anticipation of the future. On October 10, 1891, he wrote, "Some enterprising, vigorous, big-minded man will form a company some day and dam the Columbia at some place where nature makes it feasible."[23]

Another project Jackson had been asking for and predicting for years saw the light of day in 1896 with the completion of the locks at the Cascades (the present town of Cascade Locks). This put Eastern Oregon one link closer to viable, inexpensive trade with the Portland area and beyond.

While working toward the improvement of society, Jackson's sometimes caustic sense of humor worked very well:

> *Mr. Columbus Hendricks is opposing the voting of the regular annual school tax and says he will spend up to twenty dollars to defeat it. Mr. Hendricks is abundantly able to spend twenty dollars in this way. He secured many twenty dollar gold pieces from the renting of bawdy houses.*

Since his income is largely derived from this source, it is quite natural for him to expend some of it against the maintenance of public schools, which have the effect of decreasing the demand for such houses. [24]

In response to another paper's congratulations on the maiden issue when the *East Oregonian* went daily, Jackson replied:

It wasn't a maiden. A maiden is nice, sweet, lovable beyond comparison with anything on earth, and this the East Oregonian *is not. It is a boy. It intends to wear breeches and boots. It will be broad-shouldered, strong limbed and clarion voiced. It cannot sing; and may not pray much publicly, but has an arm with a fist on the end of it, and its boot is propelled by no "maiden" muscles.* [25]

Toward the end of his stay in Pendleton, Jackson became one of the six men who dreamed up the (now world-renowned) Pendleton Round-Up.

But Sam Jackson was too good for small-town Pendleton. By the time of the construction of the Columbia River Highway, we find Jackson in Portland publishing the *Portland Journal*. He was to become one of the foremost proponents of the scenic highway through the Gorge of the Columbia.

5
SIMON BENSON

TIMBER BARON

S imon Benson came to the Northwest from Norway by way of Wisconsin. Born Simon Iversen in September 1851 in the village of Gausdal, he had only a few years in the local grade school before coming to the United States in his teens.

Benson's eldest brother, Jon, had been sent to the New World in 1861. As was the custom, Jon, who began spelling his name "John," found work and saved to send for the next eldest child in the family.

Eventually, they were able to send for the rest of the family, and in 1867, fifteen-year-old Simon, his mother and father and the other four siblings sailed from Norway to New York. The trip took five weeks. Simon soon found farm work and labored sixteen-hour days to pay his brother back for his passage.

The Bensons became Americans both in name and in spirit. Many years later, Simon summed up the philosophy of the entire family:

> *I believe that foreigners who come to this country should simplify their names for the sake of their children, and that they should become Americans, not in name only but in heart also. They should learn to read and write in the tongue of their adopted country as soon as possible and they should become citizens, for I believe that if this country isn't good enough to become a citizen of, it is too good for a foreigner to stay here and make his living in.*[26]

Simon's employer, a far-sighted man, had promised a two-dollar-per-month bonus if Simon would learn to speak English. At the end of his first

Simon Benson, who said, "No successful person is afraid to work." *Courtesy of Oregon Historical Society.*

three months, he was richer by six dollars, and he could speak his new language, at least well enough to be understood. He also attended school in the evenings for a short time.

At the age of seventeen, Simon began working in a logging camp in the winter and a sawmill in the summer. He married Esther Searle when he was twenty-five and opened a general store, which was destroyed by fire only three years later.

With no insurance, and a wife and son—Amos, born in 1877—to support, Simon decided to move to the Oregon country to see if he could make a success there. He said, "Losing your money doesn't amount to anything, so long as you don't lose your courage."[27]

It was perfect timing. The lumber industry in the Midwest was beginning to wane, but in the Pacific Northwest, it was on the rise. Simon had heard that the area around Portland, Oregon, was rich in timber and ripe for the man who knew what to do about it. He'd had plenty of experience in the forests of Wisconsin and wanted to find similar work in the Pacific Northwest. He managed to find enough money for the family's passage to Portland, and they arrived soon afterward.

He left his wife and son at a hotel and found a job near the village of St. Helens on the south bank of the Columbia. Benson found that the lumbering methods used in the Northwest were unlike what he was used to in Wisconsin, as the land and climate were quite different. When he discovered that because of the high water content of the ground, logs could not be "yarded" by the methods familiar to him, he learned to make skid roads for hauling the logs out of the forest.

In two months, he was able to send for Esther and Amos. The following spring, he purchased 160 acres of prime timberland containing 6 million feet of timber. Only three years later, he was able to pay off the total price and all operating expenses and show a profit as well. In addition, he owned three yoke of oxen and had some money in the bank.

But soon, another setback occurred. Simon's wife, Esther, had never been well. She developed tuberculosis. He sold out and moved with her and the children—baby Alice had joined Amos—to the town of Colfax in eastern Washington, a much drier climate. Benson sold his quarter section along with his oxen and logging equipment for $6,000 and took a job as a foreman in a Colfax sawmill at $75 per month. Esther, hoping to help, opened a small millinery store, but even with this additional income, the family was very short on cash. Eventually, the Bensons' savings were depleted. In 1888, Simon returned to logging, leaving his wife and children (who now numbered three) in the care of others until he could return.

Benson's new location was twenty miles downriver from the land he had logged before, at a place called Beaver Creek. During logging season, Benson and his crew lived in small wooden shacks in the woods. Simon did all the cooking for himself and his four loggers. Unfortunately, that first spring, the water in the creeks was not high enough or powerful enough to wash down the timber he had cut. The logs jammed. Unable and unwilling to wait any longer, he left the logs where they were, sold his oxen and returned to eastern Washington for a visit with his family.

Returning to Beaver Creek the next season, he set out yet again to make a success of himself—a goal he thought quite attainable. This time, he contracted to buy timber and sell it to another company. In two years, he was able to pay off all his debts.

In 1891 came a turning point in Simon's life. Esther Searle Benson, his wife of sixteen years, died. The children were ages fourteen, ten and seven. Funeral and doctor bills ate up Simon's savings, and his life would never be the same.

The loss of his wife was not something that could be fixed by hard work or determination. But at age thirty-nine, Simon Benson knew from experience that giving up was not an option. With his younger children safely in the care of others, Simon returned with his firstborn, Amos, to the Lower Columbia.

Benson found a tract of timberland he wanted. Although he had no money, his credit was excellent. He arranged for the purchase price and start-up costs. His operation was highly successful, and he soon added another tract of land near Deep River, about thirty miles from Cathlamet. He was not above working with his men in any kind of job. He set the standard to which they were expected to rise. And they did.

He built the Northwest's first railroad into timberland in 1891. In Portland, he purchased two engines and some second-hand steel rails. He set himself up to move timber out to the river. But the nation was heading into a time of depression, and the price of lumber fell by a third.

Maintaining his optimism, Simon bought out two competitors and purchased two more engines and a locomotive. His confidence was well placed, as eventually the market improved, and he was, by this time, way ahead of the competition. He organized and was the first president of the Benson Logging & Lumber Company.

On Christmas Day 1895, Simon remarried. His new wife, Pamelia Loomis, presented him in due time with two more sons.

The lumber business was booming in the Northwest at this time. Benson worked his way to the top of the industry at a time when innovation was changing the face of lumbering. He worked first with oxen and later with a donkey engine. The donkey, an engine powered by steam, had not been thought feasible in the damp forests of the Northwest, but Simon Benson made it work.

As the methods of sawmilling changed and streamlined, the methods of getting the raw lumber out of the woods and to the sawmills were forced to keep pace. And Simon Benson was at the forefront of logging modernization. He became an inventor out of necessity, creating new ways to use machines to help harvest his timber.

Benson gradually sold off his oxen in the last half of the 1890s, replacing them with donkey engines at a time when other logging operations had yet to figure out how to use them successfully. With his profits he bought more timberland, logging equipment and railroad materials to reach deep into his ever-expanding empire. He kept close track of his books and continued to prosper.

One of the reasons for this was his reputation for top-quality lumber. He was able to charge more than others because the quality of his lumber was better. And he made use of that newfangled contraption, the telephone, to keep his finger on the pulse of his operations.

In 1896, forest fire threatened one of Benson's operations, the Oak Point Camp in Cowlitz County, Washington. When the wind changed and the threat became obvious, he led all the people—about 150 of them, including his own family—to safety. He took them along a cliff above the river to a rope ladder and then down the ladder to the Columbia. His own calm demeanor set the standard. No one panicked, and no one was injured.

In 1898, he moved his family to Portland, leaving his eldest son, Amos, in Washington to oversee the work.

One of Benson's famous cigar rafts, holding between 4 and 6 million board feet of lumber. *Courtesy of David Sell.*

Probably Benson's most innovative idea was his cigar-shaped log raft. Normally, many logs were lost on the ocean voyage from Portland or downriver ports to mills in California, when the traditionally designed log rafts broke up at sea. These rafts were made up of a number of floating logs, surrounded by a chained-together log "fence." But if the seas were rough, individual logs could easily wash over the side, or the chained logs could be separated, thus freeing the entire load.

Benson's log raft, taking about four to seven weeks to construct, was built in a "crib." It was chained together in a self-tightening configuration, eliminating the tendency for the mass to loosen. The first raft was six hundred feet long, fifty-five feet wide and seventeen feet above sea level, with a draft of twenty-eight feet. It contained 250 tons of chain. Its basic shape was very similar to today's great ocean liners. This first raft contained about 4 million board feet of lumber. Later rafts contained up to 6 million board feet. Benson risked a fortune in the rafting venture—and won.

Having become one of the most productive lumbermen in the Pacific Northwest, he began to turn his attention to public service. He may not have known all the directions this public spirit would take him, but the big plan for the Columbia River Highway was moving forward. And Simon Benson was going to be a part of it.

6

JOHN B. YEON

PRINCE OF THE WOODS

John Yeon was a French Canadian from Ontario. He was born Jean Baptiste Yeon in 1865 to a hardworking farm family.

At the age of seventeen, with his parents' permission, he traveled to the United States to find work. He spoke no English, but by keeping quiet and listening, he soon learned the new language. His first job was in Ohio, where he signed on as a team driver for a logging operation. He asked his employer to bank his paychecks for him, thinking it would be a good way to save his money rather than spending it. Unfortunately, the business went bankrupt, and he never received his pay for the six months he had worked. It was a hard way to learn the lesson, but from that time on, he made a point of taking care of his own money.

Even though Yeon lost his money, he learned a few things about logging. He worked for a short time for another logger and then headed for the Pacific Northwest. He did not have the four dollars needed for the last leg of his journey from Astoria to a logging camp on the Columbia, so he offered to work on the boat to earn his passage.

His work at the lumber camp involved digging ditches, cutting brush and clearing the woods for the logging operation. It was hard work and paid less than the job he really wanted. Apparently, his work spoke well of him. When he requested a job as a teamster, he was promoted, and within a week, he filled in for the head teamster, who failed to show up for work one day. Yeon was handling a seven-yoke team (fourteen oxen) and got out two logs more than anyone in the camp had ever done before. In the next few days,

John Yeon. *Courtesy of David Sell.*

he added five more logs to the record. He proved so valuable that he was hired for the head teamster position at one hundred dollars a month.

While many loggers lived on their earnings through the winter until logging began again in the spring, John Yeon made use of the winter months by working at other jobs so his money would not be all gone by the spring. In only a few years, he had saved $1,200 and was serving as camp foreman. He invested in a small piece of timberland and started his own logging company. "As fast as I made any money I put it back into timber," he said. "My biggest asset was that I knew every detail of the lumber business."[28]

The work ethic that he had learned as a farm child in Ontario continued to serve Yeon into his adult life. He was quoted in a newspaper article as saying:

The secret of my success lay in the fact that during dull seasons I did not close down my camps like most of the loggers did, but kept at work, keeping my equipment in shape and assembling my logs so that when good times came again I was ready to put my logs on the market and get the top price.[29]

In the logging business, Yeon wore many hats. He was sometimes the foreman, timekeeper or bullwhacker, and occasionally, he was even the cook. He was very careful about how he spent his money, buying only the best, knowing that less expensive and poorly made items would break or wear out faster than the better-quality ones. He made sure the men in his camp were fed the very best food available; men who are happy and healthy will work better than men who aren't.

And he was willing to invest money—a lot of money if needed—to make his operation more successful. At one point, he built a stone and masonry dam costing $9,000—a huge investment in his day—to hold back spring run-off until it was needed to float his logs down to the Columbia and to market. It was very successful and paid for itself several times over.

Eventually, Yeon sold his lumbering business and considered retiring. But after only a few months, he just couldn't stand being out of the business and bought another tract of timber.

John Yeon, roadmaster of the Columbia River Highway. *Courtesy of David Sell.*

By 1905, John Yeon's focus was changing. Knowing that he would soon sell his logging business (for the second time), Yeon moved into Portland and began buying real estate. Some people thought it foolish when he bought the lot diagonally across from Meier and Frank's huge department store, intending to erect a large office building there. But he was confident that the town's growth would prove it a wise decision. He was right.

He visited several cities to study the large buildings there. He wanted to select the best features for his own building.[30] Yeon, true to his nature, became actively involved in the construction of his building. Just as he had learned the logging business, he now learned about construction.

7

HENRY WEMME

EAGER AUTOMOBILE OWNER

Henry Wemme owned the first automobile in the city of Portland. Born Ernest Henry Wemme in Crostau, Saxony, this young man with only a grade school education immigrated to the United States when he was nineteen, perhaps to avoid enrollment in the German army. He had no intention of staying.

Unfortunately, he went broke. Unable to pay his way home or to find work as a flour miller, the trade in which he had apprenticed, he worked at any job he could find for several years. He ended up doing a number of things he hadn't been trained for—things like clearing empty beer glasses from tables, washing bottles or unloading wood from railroad cars. Through no fault of his own, he usually wound up not getting paid for these jobs.

Finally, he got a job stringing telegraph wires. He didn't know what he was doing but soon caught on. Later, he got a job doing inside wiring. When that job ended, he optimistically applied for a position as an expert electrician. Again, he didn't know what he was doing but soon learned. Unfortunately, his boss on that job suffered mental problems and was sent to an insane asylum. So Wemme lost his job, again.

Because he'd had such bad luck supporting himself working for others, Wemme decided to start his own sign-hanging business. Again he met with misfortune—he fell from the top of a six-story building on which he was working. Fortunately, the rope he had tied around his waist held firm. But while he was dangling at the end of the rope, he decided rather quickly to change his line of work.

Next, Wemme took on the job of steamfitter, another job for which he was totally unqualified. When the boss discovered the depth of his ignorance, he was promptly fired.

Deciding to try his luck in the Pacific Northwest, Wemme moved in that direction. He stopped in Helena, Montana, for a time. He told a hotel proprietor he was an expert cook. This resulted in his peeling potatoes and shelling peas for several months. But by watching and asking questions, he gradually became a decent cook.

Wemme was certainly not a quitter. He eventually decided to put himself in the business of sewing up rips in awnings, which in turn, led to the beginning of a tent-manufacturing venture. He planned to provide tents and supplies to men headed for the Klondike gold rush. Unfortunately (a word all too often associated with Wemme's ventures), the Alaska boom was screeching to a halt just as Wemme received a huge order for canvas and cotton.

But for once, luck was on his side. The USS *Maine* was sunk (February 15, 1898) in Havana Harbor, and within the year, the Spanish-American War was on. Hospital tents were needed—thirty-two thousand hospital tents, to be exact, plus an open order for all he could make. And Wemme, who possessed more tent-making materials than all other West Coast dealers combined, was swimming in profits.

In 1899, Wemme made a decision that took him in a whole new direction. He decided to buy an automobile. At this time, no one in Portland owned such a thing. Most people had not even heard of this newfangled invention and were quite content with horses and buggies or wagons pulled by mules or oxen.

But not Henry Wemme: he wanted an automobile. The streets in Portland were nothing but dust in the summer and mud in the winter, but he wasn't worried. It was no matter that an automobile cost a lot of money or that every single other person in Portland found the old mode of travel just fine. Henry Wemme wanted an automobile. So he bought one.

He purchased his first car from the Stanley brothers in Newton, Massachusetts. It was a good little machine, and he liked it a lot. However, the automobile had a habit of bouncing its driver right out onto the road if he tried to go more than ten miles an hour.

Wemme himself—even without his noisy machines—was quite a character:

As for his personality, Wemme usually dressed like a poverty-stricken laborer. He seldom wore pressed clothes or had his shoes shined and he was generally unshaven. He was always mouthing an unlighted cigar, the liquid qualities of which ran down both sides of his mouth and chin. He worked like a horse and lived like a hermit.[31]

Wemme, who never married, was also the owner of the second automobile in Portland. Having sold the little Stanley to someone in Spokane, he next purchased a Haynes-Apperson from Kokomo, Indiana. He also was the owner of the first Reo, the first Oldsmobile, the first Thomas Flyer and the first Pierce Arrow in Portland. He was the first president of the Portland Automobile Association.

In 1906, a man by the name of Max Hirsch sold his $50,000 worth of stock in the Meier and Frank department store and used his money to purchase Wemme's tent-making business. He took on a business partner, and they became known as Hirsch-Weis. Later, the company was bought again and came to be known by a name we still recognize today: White Stag.

Wemme, once his early days were behind him, invested much of his wealth in downtown Portland real estate.

The tiny community of Wemme, just to the west of Mount Hood, is easily overlooked today as folks drive past on the highway either to or from their stay at Mount Hood and its villages. With the highway being four lanes and nearly as straight as an arrow, it is hardly an indication of the early day horrors of the Barlow Trail (and later the Barlow Toll Road).

This excellent road is partially a result of that enthusiastic automobile owner Henry Wemme. He purchased the road in 1912 for $5,400. After spending $25,000 of his own money on much-needed improvements, he eliminated the toll and opened the road to free travel. Upon his death, the road was willed to Wemme's attorney, George W. Joseph, and it was held in a trust until it was accepted by the Oregon Highway Commission in 1919 to be developed into the Mount Hood Loop Highway that we enjoy today.

Henry Wemme died in 1914, before the completion of the Columbia River Highway. After the usual political wrangling over his will, half his estate went to "found and maintain a large home for wayward girls."[32] This Salvation Army White Shield Home in Portland provides services for pregnant teens and young unwed mothers.

8

Margaret E. Henderson

Hostess Extraordinaire

Margaret Elisabeth Darling was born in a pretty little valley just a short distance east of Portland in 1872 to homesteading parents. Her father was an accomplished woodworker, making cabinets and doing wood finishing. He also did finishing work and repair on steamboats and other vessels.

Margaret was only fifteen when she married twenty-seven-year-old Harry Hackett. He was a boat captain on both the Columbia and Willamette Rivers and had operated ferryboats as well. He had also, for a time, worked as a fireman on the Oregon Railroad and Navigation Line.

Harry and Margaret Hackett had a son, Henry, and a daughter, Lavina. In 1891, the year Lavina was born, Harry moved to the Hood River Valley to develop an orchard. There is no mention of his bringing his wife and children with him; it seems that he left them behind.

Some time later, Margaret married a Mr. Newell, also a riverboat captain. We don't know when or why this marriage ended, but in 1910, she married John Leland Henderson.

Henderson, for a change, was not a riverboat captain. He was different in many ways from Margaret's first two husbands. He had been a schoolteacher in California and Oregon. He had been county surveyor, justice of the peace and Portland city engineer and was practicing law at the time he married Margaret. People referred to him as "Judge" Henderson.

Strangely, or perhaps predictably, this husband seems to have vanished like the others. He was fifty-nine at the time of their marriage in 1910; perhaps he died. From 1911 on, he is never mentioned again in written accounts of

Margaret Elisabeth Henderson, roadhouse queen of the Columbia River Gorge. *Courtesy of Friends of Vista House.*

Margaret's very interesting life. But Henderson is the name she kept for her remaining years.

Perhaps it is partly because of Margaret's failed marriages that she felt the need to develop her abilities and make her own way in the world.

Left with no husband to support her at a time in our history when most women stayed at home working to create a nurturing environment and raising their children, Margaret needed to find a way to support herself. She had studied art for a short time in Portland and applied first to Meier and Frank's in Portland, where she was hired to decorate windows at the store. Soon, she also began working as a waitress in their popular lunchroom.

9
"MAJOR" HENRY L. BOWLBY

Henry L. Bowlby was kicked out of West Point. Born on the last day of 1879, young Henry entered the U.S. Military Academy at age eighteen, probably anticipating an illustrious career in the military. But a childish prank terminated his time there. Whether he actually participated in the shenanigans in the mess hall was never the question. He was called on the carpet for standing in support of those who were involved. It was a breach of military discipline, and in the spring of 1901, he and his fellow miscreants were officially expelled.

Deciding Ecuador might be a good place to lick his wounds and figure out what to do next with his life, he and a few of the others traveled there and got work laying out railroads. It was a perfect opportunity for this talented young man to develop his knowledge and experience.

When the group returned to the States in 1904, they refused, en masse, an offer of a military commission from President Theodore Roosevelt. (This detail did not, however, prevent Bowlby from adding the title of "Major" to his name.) Instead, he picked up his studies at the University of Nebraska, where he earned a bachelor's degree and also a graduate degree in civil engineering.

In 1905, he was accepted at the University of Washington as an instructor under Sam Lancaster. By 1908, he was working with Lancaster on formulating curriculum.

With the help of Sam Hill, he became Washington State's highway commissioner. He did a good job building a modern highway department in the state, but not all the state's citizens wanted what he had to offer. The legislature did not support him, and the governor chose to ignore the problem. Bowlby needed a place where he could do what he had been trained to do. The time would come soon.

10

OSWALD WEST

A FUTURE GOVERNOR

Os West, as he was known, was born in Canada but came to Salem in 1877 at the age of four. Nothing in his family's circumstances hinted of a future career in government, but a lazy-day encounter with a couple unbroken horses changed all that. Os and his brother decided, with all the wisdom of youth, to hitch a pair of wild horses to a nearby wagon and drive them south on Commercial Street and up the steep hill there. After the expected challenge of getting the animals hitched, Os pulled off their blindfolds and scrambled aboard the wagon with his brother at the reins. According to the story he wrote about the adventure a couple years later, the horses were "bucking and bellowing" and sometimes on the same side of the wagon tongue.[33] But by the time the animals reached the top of the hill, they were subdued enough to turn and pull the wagon home with the utmost politeness.

When Asahel Bush, one of the owners of the Ladd and Bush Bank of Salem, heard the story, he decided this was a young man who showed promise and offered Os a job carrying messages for the bank. West had entered a new world—one peopled by the wealthy, the respected and the leaders of the future. And it rubbed off on him.

By the time he was promoted to teller, he knew enough to realize that his books needed to balance at the end of the day. When presented, one day, with a check for $2,750, he paid it—and then had second thoughts. After all, $2,750 was a lot of money, and how was he to know whether the man had funds to cover the check? He left the bank, checked with the presenter's attorney and promptly decided action was needed. Here is his account of the incident:

> *I lost no time in grabbing my hat and six shooter. I was able to head the gentleman off before he caught his train. I backed him into a nearby saloon. I made him straddle a whiskey barrel, went through his pockets, recovered the loot, and was able to balance my cash that night.*[34]

West may have had a few rough edges, but he certainly would not cringe in the face of difficulty.

Bush continued to mold the young man, teaching and encouraging him. He felt politics was calling Os West. And who was West to argue?

There was one small problem. Os West was an outdoorsman. He hated being closed in an office. He could bear it for a time, but then he just needed open spaces. His early adult life is a patchwork of office work and the great outdoors. At age twenty-four, he married Mabel Hutton. Still not quite ready to abandon his gipsy ways, he went for two years to the Yukon to search for gold.

In 1903, he was appointed the Oregon State land agent. He saw the appointment as an opportunity for public service. In these early days, many people did pretty much what they wanted to without repercussions. But times were changing. West confronted land barons who had stolen thousands of acres of forestland from the state. These lands were intended to support the state's schools, and West intended to see that happen.

Although he probably didn't realize it, all these experiences were slowly shaping him into a man who was greatly needed when it came time to build a highway through the Gorge of the Columbia.

11
JULIUS MEIER

LAWYER, MERCHANT, ANOTHER FUTURE GOVERNOR

Aaron Meier, a German Jew, had immigrated to this country in 1855. His first "store" consisted of assorted bits of merchandise in a pack on his back, which he peddled in the rural areas south of Portland. But by the time he was twenty-six, Aaron Meier had rented a building in Portland and was beginning to develop a reputation as a merchant and worthy citizen of that great city.

Aaron's son, Julius, was born in Portland in 1874. In 1895, he graduated from the University of Oregon Law School. Meier did not have a middle name, but when the sign painter assured him that all good lawyers had one, Meier suggested a middle initial *L*. And after that, he was always known as Julius L. Meier.

Meier traveled with his family to Bavaria (a state in southeast Germany) as a young man, bringing back pictures in his mind of the wonderful public works there.

After four years of practicing law, Meier joined the family business—the Meier and Frank department store.

Julius was working with his father in the business when he was married to Grace Mayer on Christmas Day 1901. In 1910, he became general manager of Meier and Frank. His leadership skill grew with practice and prepared him for the Columbia River Highway's construction. And in turn, it was partly his experience in promoting the highway that prepared him for future government service.

As the first decade of the twentieth century drew to a close, farmers, riders of bicycles, auto enthusiasts and engineers were focusing more and more on the need for good roads. It was only a matter of time until their hopes were realized.

PART 2

ON YOUR MARK, GET SET...

12

LIVES INTERSECTING

D estiny is sometimes so obvious in retrospect.
Sam Hill, Sam Lancaster, Simon Benson, John Yeon and all the others—they were all in the right place at the right time.

In 1909, the Alaska-Pacific-Yukon Exposition was to take place in Seattle, and the meeting of the first American Congress of Road Builders was to be part of the event. Hill, of course, played a major role in the festivities, providing for the delegates a trip by ferry to Canada's Vancouver Island in addition to his usual fare of speeches and magic lantern shows. He promoted both a north–south highway on the west side of the Cascade Mountains and a highway on the Washington (north) side of the Columbia River, connecting the more populous western part of the state to the east side—and incidentally, to Sam's property and unfinished mansion. He seemed to be making good progress in this effort. Unfortunately, even Ernest Lister, whom Hill had supported as the good roads candidate for the office of governor, once elected, declined to go along with Hill's plan.

Not to be thwarted, Hill turned his attention to Oregon. He moved into the Arlington Club in Portland and opened his Home Telegraph and Telephone Company.

Henry Bowlby was still in Washington State. The few paved roads at this time were water-bound macadam (crushed rock), which worked well with the iron wagon tires but was not appropriate for automobiles. And unfortunately, the tar or asphalt roads designed for automobile traffic did not hold up well to the traffic of horses and iron-tired wagons. Still, recognizing the changing needs of transportation, Bowlby had begun designing and paving roads specifically for the automobile.

In 1907, at age forty-two, John Yeon married Elizabeth Welsh. Elizabeth's family, prominent in the Portland social scene, made him aware of opportunities to improve the public good. He began purchasing properties and also looking for opportunities to serve.

In August 1910, he began construction on a large office building in Portland—a building most people said was way too ambitious. At fifteen stories high (the tallest skyscraper in Portland) and a full city block, people thought it was just too much building and that Yeon would never find enough tenants to make it financially successful. But Yeon had read the needs of the city correctly and planned wisely. By the time the building was ready for occupancy on February 1, 1911, every one of the 365 offices was rented.

Simon Benson, after a 1910 trip up the Mount Hood Highway, turned his thoughts to the subject of roads. This "highway" was nothing but mud and steep hills. Often farmers brought horses to pull the cars out of the mire. In fact, some farmers had been known to hollow out the low places in the roads, knowing they'd have business after every hearty rain. Benson knew it was time for progress to take over.

An auto being rescued from the mud by teams of horses or mules was not an uncommon sight in the early years of the twentieth century. *Courtesy of the Virginia Historical Society.*

On Your Mark, Get Set...

In 1910, Henry Wemme joined with Lewis Russell, a Portland auto enthusiast, to circulate a petition promoting a road from Bridal Veil Falls to the Hood River County line. The idea was approved, and in May of that year, Philo Holbrook, the county surveyor, mapped out a road with hairpin turns and very steep grades. In 1912, a portion of this road was constructed, beginning at Bridal Veil and heading east for almost two miles. The road was not only steep and winding but also encountered right-of-way problems with the railroad.

Another bit of "road" between Chanticleer Point and Latourell Falls was a rough track with grades of up to 22 percent. Holbrook attempted to plot a better road here as well but gave up in despair. He said it couldn't be done, even allowing a 12 percent grade. The effort, while not resulting in a useable highway, was one more step in the right direction.

Sam Hill brought Sam Lancaster from Seattle to Maryhill and assigned him the monumental task of building experimental roads, especially a road from the Columbia River up the steep hills toward the town of Goldendale. Lancaster saw it as the perfect opportunity to try out various road-building methods and test them for durability. The road was in one specific climate zone, and it would have pretty much the same amount of traffic for its entire length, thus allowing for

The Maryhill Loops Road. *Photo by the author.*

comparisons between sections constructed to various standards. Here Lancaster also refined his theory of reducing grade by developing distance.

If a distance between two points had to rise four hundred feet in only one mile, for example, Lancaster designed a longer road with sweeping curves, extending its length and thus allowing a gentle 5 percent grade. He kept accurate records of methods and materials in order to determine what worked—and what didn't. A failed road was not considered a failure. It was instead an example of what not to do in the future. It was at this time, also, that Lancaster designed several machines to minimize the manpower needed to construct roads.

While some of Lancaster's correspondence during this time was handwritten in a calligraphic script with the flowery phrases associated with the era, other missives were typed by a secretary and now appear similar to text messages in terms of brevity and lack of concern for style, grammar and punctuation.

Several of his letters contain hand drawings of machines or machine parts along with measurements. He was involved not only in designing the location of the road but also in its construction materials and even with the machines that would accomplish the job.

Records seem to indicate that Lancaster was busy from dawn till dusk arranging all the details of the road's construction. He also designed and built a dam near the road in an attempt to provide a water reservoir for the town below. The dam failed within a year. But Hill had the means to allow Lancaster to try things, and it was a good learning experience.

In March 1911, Henry Bowlby resigned—under pressure—from his position as highway commissioner in Washington State.

In 1912, Margaret Henderson left Meier and Frank's, sold her house, took her recently gained knowledge of food service and joined Mr. and Mrs. A.R. Morgan in a business venture that forms an important part of the Columbia River Highway story. Together, they opened Chanticleer Inn. Almost immediately, Chanticleer earned a place in the hearts of Portland's elite. Margaret had a real flair for creating a welcoming and relaxing atmosphere. She also cooked an outstanding chicken dinner.

Chanticleer, named for the rooster in Chaucer's *Canterbury Tales*, was situated atop a cliff above the euphemistically named Rooster Rock on the Columbia. Visitors took the train or steamboat from Portland to Rooster Rock Landing. From there, they walked up a very steep dirt trail to Chanticleer at the top of the bluff. It was quite an adventure.

But getting to Chanticleer was not only an adventure. Sometimes it was a real pain in the neck. On more than one occasion, Margaret climbed the road in the snow carrying supplies on her back. And sometimes people were

Chanticleer Inn. *Photo by Pacific Photo Company, courtesy of Old Oregon.*

The *Hattie Belle*, stern-wheeler, at Rooster Rock in 1896. *A Gifford penny postcard, author's collection.*

marooned there for days at a time. Chanticleer Inn was just about perfect in every way but one—it needed a good road. Margaret haunted the offices of Portland highway officials promoting her cause.

In early 1912, Sam Hill took Henry Bowlby, two Multnomah County commissioners, the Multnomah County surveyor and the road superintendent on a two-day trip in the Gorge east of Portland. The men traveled on foot to search for a possible route between Portland and Cascade Locks. It was not an easy trip, sometimes requiring ropes to move from one point to another, but even Henry Pittock, now in his seventies, gamely tagged along. The journey had its intended outcome—Sam Hill was encouraged to pursue his dream road in Oregon.

Sam Lancaster, in December of that year, traveled to Washington, D.C., to lobby for the completion of a road system at Mount Rainier National Park in Washington State.

Simon Benson had more than fulfilled the dreams of his youth, becoming a wealthy man by working hard, trying new ideas and always doing the right thing. He was ready to spend money, rather than earn it, to do things that would make Portland and Oregon a better place to live. In 1912, he began a decade of public service. One of his first projects became known as "Benson's Bubblers." Feeling that saloons "produced nothing of value and were parasites on legitimate industry,"[35] Benson decided to pipe good, pure water to Portland street corners and provide public drinking fountains (of bronze, no less!) for the people of the city. His hope that men who had easy access to good water would not be so eager to frequent the saloons was fulfilled, as saloons reported up to a 40 percent drop in business. And Benson moved on to other projects.

This same year, he began building the Benson Hotel in Portland. He was optimistic about tourism and wanted to promote it. The hotel, complete with an ice water tap in each room, opened in March 1913.

Benson had long been aware of what good roads could do for the area. He had seen many beautiful but inaccessible areas during his logging years and had taken a steamer up the Columbia River many times, always considering the transportation possibilities a good road along the bank of the river could open up. In 1912, he decided to see if a stable road could be constructed across Shellrock Mountain—a loose talus slope that had been the bane of travelers since recorded history of the area. He encouraged Oregon's governor Os West to attempt a road across the slippery rock using prison labor and put up $10,000 toward the effort.

The road began destroying itself almost as soon as it was completed. But Benson didn't consider it a failure. Its value lay in the education derived from the exercise. The attempt had proven one thing beyond a doubt—hard work wasn't enough; expert engineering was required as well.

While the road itself did not meet Benson's expectations, it did serve to increase the fervor of Multnomah County road enthusiasts.

PART 3

GO! CONSTRUCTING THE HIGHWAY

13

1913

In February 1913, Sam Hill invited Governor Os West and the entire Oregon legislature (and, consequently, the press) to visit "his" town of Maryhill. The purpose of the trip was to show Oregon how to get out of the mud. The eighty-eight men met in Portland at Hill's Home Telephone and Telegraph Company at five o'clock in the morning and then drove to Vancouver Washington, taking a ferry across the river. In Vancouver, they boarded the special railroad car Hill had commissioned for the trip. The train was well supplied with food and drink, and everyone arrived at Maryhill in good humor despite the February weather.

Sam preached the value of good roads with an impassioned fervor, showed his hand-tinted magic lantern slides to the men and took them to personally meet and admire his $100,000 Maryhill Loops road. They were mightily impressed.

According to Hill's biographer, "The legislature's resolution of thanks for the excursion and '...the unselfish work that is being done by Mr. Hill in the cause of good roads'" was only one of the alcohol-inspired resolutions extolling the virtues of Mr. Hill.[36]

The resolution itself meant nothing. It was action Hill wanted. And he got it. The legislators returned to Salem and promptly formed the Oregon State Highway Commission. Hill insisted the commission members hire Henry L. Bowlby as state engineer, and they did. The commission, however, was broke and without power. Only a small appropriation was made for office expenses; no monies were made available for the actual construction of roads. The practical cost for the building of roads, it seemed, was to be borne by the counties.

In the early years of the twentieth century, automobiles had made great inroads into the culture of America, but they were still considered toys for the rich. Ordinary people, for the most part, thought them a nuisance. Some were offended by their presence.

But momentum in the public sector was picking up steam. The *Oregonian* (Henry Pittock) and the *Journal* (Sam Jackson) were unflagging in their support of a highway through the Gorge. The Columbia Highway Association, with Julius Meier as president, worked to promote the construction of a highway all the way from Astoria at the mouth of the Columbia to The Dalles—and perhaps even as far as Pendleton. Benson and other influential citizens encouraged Multnomah and Hood River County residents. They backed the enterprise in every way possible.

Henry Ford introduced America to his most famous automobile, the Model T, when he began production in 1908. In 1913, he introduced the moving assembly line, which meant more cars with fewer workers and within a shorter time span. At the 1908 price of $850, they were still much too dear for the average buyer, but by 1913, 200,000 Model Ts were produced and sold at a price of around $500. They had become an affordable item—much like home computers one hundred years later.

Sam Hill must have been chomping at the proverbial bit during all this. What was taking so long? Didn't these people realize that summer was passing them by—day by day? Didn't they understand that bad weather and road construction were pretty much mutually exclusive? This highway should have been started yesterday!

Continuing, at a pace brisk enough for most people, on July 26, 1913, the Multnomah County commissioners, under the leadership of chairman Rufus C. Holman, appointed a committee to advise them on matters connected with the new departure in modern road building. Included on the five-member committee were Amos Benson (Simon's eldest son), Sam Jackson and Sam Hill.

The moving of bureaucracy may have been slower than Hill and some others wanted it, but finally, the critical day arrived: Wednesday, August 27, 1913. This was the day things really started popping. And Margaret Henderson got to be a part of it.

Sam Hill hosted the luncheon meeting that day at Chanticleer Inn. Included were Multnomah County's new Advisory Board on Roads and Highways as well as the county commissioners and local backers: Bowlby,

Chanticleer's reception room, a place of beauty and peace created by Margaret Henderson. *Courtesy of David Sell.*

Simon Benson, Sam Jackson, Henry Pittock, John Yeon, Henry Wemme, Margaret Henderson and several others. Hill also brought along his protégée, Sam Lancaster.

After a delightful chicken dinner, the men adjourned to the parlor to discuss business. They agreed to begin construction on the automobile highway through the Gorge of the Columbia. The commissioners' decision to move forward was unanimous. It was one of those magic moments when preparation met opportunity.

At the end of the meeting, Sam Hill turned to their hostess. "Mrs. Henderson," he announced with his usual pomp, "you shall have your highway!"

14
MULTNOMAH COUNTY

CLIFFS AND WATERFALLS

At the Chanticleer meeting, Hill recommended Lancaster as locating engineer for the county. Lancaster had already suggested a twenty-four-foot road width—eighteen feet of paved road, with a three-foot macadamized shoulder on each side—a maximum 5 percent grade and a standard turning radius of at least two hundred feet. Commissioner Lightner objected. He felt Philo Holbrook, the current county surveyor, could do the job for far less money. But the next day, Lancaster was hired over Lightner's objections, and the commissioners voted to turn over $75,000 to the new Oregon Highway Commission for surveys and preliminary work.

It was reported that "a certain banker" said he would "favor increasing the county tax if we only had a practical business man, say like John B. Yeon, for roadmaster."[37] The remark was conveyed to Yeon, who promptly dropped his plans for a European tour to come on board as county roadmaster. He served for two years at the "salary" of one dollar per year.[38]

The next day, Lancaster was out in the field with new purpose. Recognizing the lateness of the hour, with winter weather only a few short weeks away, he set to work immediately locating the highway and planning work camps at strategic points. Those strategic points were the jewels on the necklace that would lie gracefully and lightly on the land. Lancaster vowed that "none of this wild beauty should be marred where it could be prevented. The highway was so built that not one tree was felled, not one fern was crushed, unnecessarily."[39]

In Multnomah County, these beauty spots included a number of waterfalls (not all, by any means), Thor's Heights and, of course, Chanticleer Point.

Possible paths for the road to travel were explored, often requiring men to climb, crawl and even use ropes to drag themselves up the hills, between Troutdale and the Multnomah County line. The first camp for workers was established at Multnomah Falls in October 1913, and the highway location was fixed to the Hood River County line by January 1914.

By February, construction was in full swing. Amos Benson was signed on as assistant to Roadmaster Yeon, and Lancaster said to him, "If the road is completed according to plans, it will rival if not surpass anything to be found in the civilized world."[40]

A number of bridges and viaducts would be required. Once the location of the road was established, men could be put to work on the most difficult and time-consuming portions first. Construction was, of course, begun on some sections before the survey was complete. Common sense dictated that construction should begin at a place that was familiar to the people of Portland, a place they cared about. Positive publicity would remain a critical aspect of this infant miracle. Lancaster needed the voters and commissioners of Multnomah County on his side.

So he began at Multnomah Falls.

We, however, a century later, have the luxury of following the road from west to east in an orderly fashion.

TROUTDALE TO THOR'S HEIGHTS

The first thing (west to east) was to cross the Sandy River. A substantial bridge already existed here at Troutdale, built in 1912 by the county. Another bridge was located on Baseline Road, near the Portland Auto Club. But the minute strip of land along the Columbia—before dredging coughed up enough sand, silt and gravel to extend the shore in the 1930s—was already occupied by the railroad. The highway would have to ascend the heights. There was no other way.

The immediate goal was the tiny town of "Upper" Corbett, at over seven hundred feet elevation. (Another tiny village, Lower Corbett, lay at river level far below.) Lancaster followed the Sandy River at an elevation between the river and the cliffs to the east, bypassing the old "wire trail"—the route of the telegraph line—because of its steepness, and followed the Sandy a bit farther before turning toward Corbett. He was sometimes able to incorporate sections of the wire trail or local market roads. The highway had gentle curves and climbed steadily at a 5 percent grade. The automobiles would hardly work up a sweat on the gentle incline. So far, so good.

The work was done with shovels, elbow grease and, sometimes, horses. They employed a tool called a "Fresno"—the invention of a Scotsman living in Fresno, California. This flat-bottomed scraper was pulled behind horses or mules like a plow. There was also no shortage of picks, sledgehammers, shovels and wheelbarrows. Many local farmers were employed in the construction.

As the road extended a mile beyond Corbett, it led to the renowned Chanticleer Inn. Mrs. Henderson did, indeed, have her highway.

This, in itself, was looked upon as no less than a miracle. Both Margaret Henderson and Portland's elite were delighted with the new road.

Not everything went smoothly. Local folklore has it that one worker, instructed to dig a ditch leading away from the road to carry off rainwater, obligingly created a ditch leading away from the road—uphill! Thank goodness John Yeon kept his eye peeled for such difficulties and corrected errors like this.

Another interesting sidelight pertaining to this Troutdale–Corbett section of the highway is the accident that occurred at the thirty-year-old Nielson Bridge near the Auto Club on Baseline Road (later called Stark Street).

On April 25, 1914—which, incidentally, had been designated Good Roads Day—the bridge collapsed under the weight of a truck full of gravel and its five-man crew. Fortunately, the most serious injury was a broken arm. The truck had been bound for the Columbia River Highway construction. The arm belonged to Charlie Bramhall, road boss of the crew working in the Corbett area.

Just east of Chanticleer Point was "the Summit" at almost nine hundred feet. From here, although the Columbia was visible below, a road in that direction was obstructed by a piece of vertical property—a treacherous cliff. There was an existing road leading east toward the top of Larch Mountain, but Philo Holbrook, the county surveyor who had run the line from Bonneville to the eastern edge of Multnomah County, had also tried, without success, to find a route from Chanticleer to Bridal Veil by way of the Larch Mountain Road. The only "road" existing there at the time boasted a roller coaster–worthy 22 percent grade. Holbrook felt he could improve that to only 12 percent—still more than double what the new Oregon State Highway Commission had set as the maximum allowable grade. According to Holbrook, 5 percent was out of the question. It just couldn't be done.

He was right; this road was impossible.

However, Lancaster had long had his eye on Thor's Heights—a promontory 730 feet above the river with a view extending twenty miles in either direction. Getting there from Chanticleer, however, would require traversing that dastardly cliff. Lancaster relished the challenge.

Lancaster had the men blast a shelf into the face of the cliff wide enough for about a third of the roadbed. The remainder was to be supported from below. An amazing amount of fill was needed (some of which was obtained from the undercut), and it was held in place by an immense dry masonry wall constructed by Italian workers, some of whom Sam Hill had brought out from his estate in Massachusetts. The upper part of the fill was carefully hand placed.

The exact location is lost to history, but it was along this section of road that the first—and possibly only—death occurred. Mario Cerighino, one of the Italian stonemasons, was caught under the chin by a blasted rock. It broke his neck, killing him instantly.[41]

Built on the memory of Mr. Cerighino, the road hugged the cliff for a quarter of a mile until it tiptoed carefully onto Thor's Heights.

THOSE TALENTED ITALIANS AND THEIR POEM IN STONE

A number of stonemasons worked on the highway, most of them Italians. Names such as Cerighino, Santilli, Crocenzi, Monaco, Camillo, Fellici, De Cicco, Monaco and Figone crop up often in written reports.

Fred Luscher, son of Swiss immigrants living in the Bridal Veil area, remembered that two labor camps were located on the Luscher property—one American and one Italian. Fred and his brother worked on the highway; their job often included hauling rock for the masons.[42]

In April 1914, Biagio Monaco, working under C. Camillo, suffered a crushed finger. He was sent to the county hospital for treatment. When the finger did not improve, Mr. Monaco saw a private doctor, who operated but was unable to save the finger and was obliged to amputate it. His representative, Albert B. Ferrera, wrote to the county that Monaco had a wife and a number of children who were wholly dependent on him. While Mr. Ferrera acknowledged that the county was not liable, he hoped they would take a favorable view of the case. In September, the county paid Mr. Monaco $204.75, and the case did not go to court.[43]

"Guard Rocks" at the top of a stone retaining wall, work of Italian stonemasons. *Courtesy of Oregon State University.*

Luigi Crocenzi, in the same month, applied to Mike Gigliatti for a job and was offered work beginning the next day. There were several men drinking whiskey, and the foreman said, "Have a drink." They had a drink, and each paid the foreman. When it came Crocenzi's turn, he paid the foreman one dollar for eleven drinks. The foreman then said he would have to talk to the superintendent about the job. Crocenzi stayed in the tent over night and, in the morning, found that he did not have a job after all. He also saw the foreman watering down the whiskey. A formal complaint was signed with Crocenzi's mark. In July, Antonio De Cicco (perhaps a lawyer) wrote to the Multnomah County commissioners (in somewhat broken English) that several men had experienced difficulties similar to Mr. Crocenzi's—having their last dollars taken in exchange for beer or whiskey and then not receiving the job as promised. Apparently Mr. Gigliatti had been found guilty by the court a few times before. De Cicco encouraged getting rid of Gigliatti and hiring "a better man at his position that will do his duty as a Gent."[44]

Gioacchino (Jack) DiBennedetto, Italian stonemason. *Courtesy of Joanne (DiBennedetto) Burdick.*

Many of the stonemasons who worked on the highway lived in the Italian neighborhood of Portland.[45] Benny DiBenedetto recalls his father, Gioacchino (Jack), packing a lunch and heading off to work on Monday mornings to spend the week at one of the various work camps. "The men liked to be able to work together, to speak their own language, sing their native songs," said DiBenedetto. He recalls the singing and the ethnic camaraderie. Portland's Italian community doubtless included some of the masons Sam Hill had brought from Massachusetts.[46]

THOR'S HEIGHTS (CROWN POINT)

Even before receiving the go-ahead from the county commissioners, Lancaster had been speculating about the many obstacles barring the way between Portland and The Dalles.

Thor's Heights, the property just past the precarious cliff-side road, was owned by two men: Danish immigrant Lorens Lund and his wife and Osmon Royal. They called it "Thor's Heights" for the Norse god of thunder. They'd lived there long enough to know exactly how fierce this god could be—especially during the winter months.

Thor's Heights was a wonderful find for the artist, Lancaster. However, there were two problems. First of all, Thor's Heights was not large enough to encircle with a road. And secondly, the next location point along the road (eastward) was to be Latourell Falls—a drop of nearly six hundred feet in only a mile and a half as the crow flies.

This bluff, with a drop of over seven hundred feet to the Columbia River below, was obviously not a reasonable location to put a road. Except, dreamer that he was, that's exactly what Lancaster intended to do. The view was magnificent, and of course, his goal was to create not only a useable highway holding to the established tight design parameters but also a place of beauty, a parkland. He measured, paced, thought it over, measured again and decided it would work. He talked Lund and Royal into donating the land to the county for the road.

While a tight circle atop Thor's Heights would be nothing compared to the hairpin turns found on most roads of the day, it was completely unacceptable for this state-of-the-art highway on which automobiles might be expected to race along at fifteen or even twenty miles per hour.

An allowance could be made in the two-hundred-foot radius restriction for cases of great difficulty. If absolutely needed, the radius could be shortened to one hundred feet, but only if the curve was accompanied by additional road width and a reduction in grade. Lancaster decided this was the perfect place to make this exception.

Not only did Lancaster intend to build a road here, he also wanted a sidewalk around the outside edge of the road where pedestrians could view and marvel over the glory of God's creation.

To meet the adopted standard, Lancaster's road—or at least the walkway abutting it—would have to soar through the air around the point.

"Impossible!" cried the naysayers. But Lancaster just smiled, drew up the plans and told John Yeon to get to work on it.

Perhaps surprisingly, the sidewalk was created before the road itself. The workers had to be anchored by ropes while constructing the piers for the sidewalk. The supports for the outer edge of the sidewalk vary in length and rest on bedrock. The land atop the heights was left bare, but Lancaster had ideas brewing in his imagination, even at this early stage of the game.

Work camps were established at various sites along the new highway. While much of the work in the Corbett area was done by farmers who signed on as day laborers, more workers were needed. Most lumbering operations in the

The sidewalk soaring around Thor's Heights before the road itself was constructed. *Courtesy of David Sell.*

Thor's Heights nearing the end of construction. By this time, people were beginning to refer to the spot as Crown Point, or Lancaster's Crown—the lights around the perimeter being the jewels in the crown. *Courtesy of Alex Blendl.*

area shut down in November, freeing loggers to join the growing ranks of road workers. In March 1914, a camp was established for 135 workers near Chanticleer. Alex Barr (whose name is currently assigned to Alex Barr Road near Latourell) was road supervisor and camp foreman.

Five of these work camps were established in late 1913 and early 1914, most located near the railroad tracks to facilitate transportation of supplies and workers. From inception to the completion of paving in Multnomah County, about 2,200 workers participated in the highway's construction. Day laborers earned $2.25 a day, and a man with a team earned $5.00.

LATOURELL

The tiny settlement of Latourell was named for its French Canadian founder, Joseph Latourell (originally spelled Latourelle). It is one of the few places where land near the Columbia is in plentiful supply. The people here were mostly farmers, enjoying the rich bottomland. They also enjoyed Joe Latourell's fiddle playing at the occasional community dances.

In locating the road from Thor's Heights to Latourell, Lancaster's experience on the Maryhill Loops Road served him well. He stretched the mile and a half crow-flight distance to two and a half miles, allowed the highway to parallel itself five times and arrived at Latourell Falls calm and collected. In spite of an occasional "design exception," the road worked very well. The slope is so gentle that early automobiles just put-putted right along, either uphill or down, with nary a hiccup—no steep grades, no hairpin turns, no fuss and no bother. And it was beautiful.

It was also designed in such a way that it would not destroy itself. Water, that nemesis of healthy roads, was taken into account from the beginning. This section of roadway included metal-capped curbs, cement gutters,

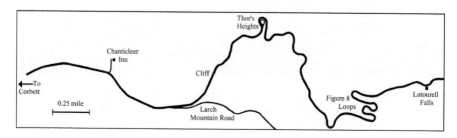

Map of the Crown Point–Latourell section of the highway. *Map by the author.*

culverts and drains designed to carry water under or away from the road. And any drainage ditches ran downhill, not up!

Latourell Falls is a 249-foot drop over columnar basalt. In fact, a person who doesn't mind getting a little wet can walk right behind it. Perhaps it made a good shower for hot workers at the end of the day. It is a beautiful location point for the highway.

But the creek below the falls is in a steep canyon, and unfortunately, the canyon walls were not adequate for supporting a bridge. Enter Karl Billner.

BRIDGES

For some parts of the highway, outside experts were hired. That's where Billner came into the picture. He was a bridge engineer, hired to design the bridge for Latourell Creek and several others as well.

Prior to the formation of the Oregon State Highway Commission, bridges were often sold to unsuspecting county courts (responsible for roads and bridges at that time) by companies more interested in making money than in providing good bridges. These cookie-cutter bridges were installed

Latourell Bridge under construction. *Courtesy of David Sell.*

The footbridge allowing Guy W. Talbot access to his land on both sides of the new highway. Note the gutter alongside the road. *Courtesy of Friends of the Historic Columbia River Highway.*

anywhere and everywhere with no consideration given to appropriate setting. They were often substandard and were costing the counties way too much in maintenance. All that was about to change.

Each bridge in the Columbia River Gorge was individually designed to enhance the natural beauty along the highway and was intended to last for a long, long time. Billner's job at Latourell was to design and build a bridge that would be secure and long lasting, even though much of the canyon's bedrock was covered with twenty-five to fifty feet of silt. This required deeply set piers and a very light structure. Billner employed reinforced concrete—the new building material of choice in the early 1900s. The deck was made in one continuous pour of thirty hours, and a sidewalk and railing were added. The cost of working in the soft base material rather than bedrock was probably offset by the savings in concrete, and the resulting bridge is both beautiful and strong. The actual construction of the bridge was awarded to the Pacific Bridge Company of Oakland, California.

The highway, here at Latourell, crossed land belonging to Guy W. Talbot. Naturally, Talbot wanted easy access to his land on both sides of the highway. So Billner designed a beautiful footbridge for him only a couple hundred feet west of the Latourell Bridge. Frank Kneiriem and Dave Butler of Corbett did the actual construction. It was known as the Talbot Bridge.

SHEPPERD'S DELL

Only a mile farther down the road was Young's Creek. George Shepperd, usually referred to as "a man of modest means," owned the property, which included the falls on Young's Creek. He called the area Shepperd's Dell. This beautiful setting had served as a place of worship for Shepperd and his family. After his wife died, Mr. Shepperd was loath to part with the land that they had loved together.

Beautiful Shepperd's Dell Bridge. *Courtesy of Oregon State University.*

When Lancaster discovered how much Shepperd loved it, he asked why he wouldn't want to share that beauty with others as well. Shepperd was convinced and gave the waterfall and the land surrounding the road to the county as a memorial to his wife.

The bridge Billner designed for this location is one of the most beautiful along the length of the highway. The footings rest on solid bedrock, and the bridge arches gracefully one hundred feet above the stream below. Lancaster designed a stairway and short trail from the bridge to a View Point near the falls.

Just past Shepperd's Dell, Lancaster blasted away part of a large basalt outcropping to squeeze the highway between the railroad track and the basalt monolith. This "half-tunnel" is known as "Bishop's Cap" or "Mushroom Rock."

BRIDAL VEIL

The next waterfall on Lancaster's itinerary was Bridal Veil. A small company town existed at this location, as well as a flume to bring logs from the Palmer Lumber Company (about a mile and a half up Larch Mountain) down to the sawmill at Bridal Veil. The flume was a significant factor in determining the location of the road. After exploring all possibilities, Lancaster and Billner determined that the bridge would have to be located almost directly above the falls. Not the most beautiful of bridges, it has solid railings—a major structural element. But it has lasted well all these years, and ultimately, at least to those who drive across it, that matters most.

Of the old company town of Bridal Veil, only the tiny post office remains. The highway passes through the present-day village of Bridal Veil and continues east, often directly adjacent to the railroad. Numerous segments of dry masonry walls and arched railings give the road a feeling of European antiquity. The walls and railings are finished in several ways depending on the natural characteristics of the rock available nearby and the whim of the mason doing the work. But all the railings have open arches, not only for appearance sake but also to facilitate water drainage.

In some places, white wooden rail fences were used instead of rock.

Mist, Wahkeena, and Multnomah

Chronologically, the first part of the road constructed was the half-mile stretch between Multnomah Falls and Gordon Creek (source of Wahkeena Falls). The road then proceeded west to Mist Falls. It was only when this much had been accomplished that a tax measure for the building and maintenance of roads was offered to the citizens of Multnomah County.

Mist Falls did not require a bridge, as it contains very little water. Instead, the moisture it brings down is handled by a culvert under the road. The waterfall, itself, usually appears only as a mist drifting from the heights to the river below—thus its name. Only at the time of the spring freshet does an actual stream of water pour over the cliff. And even then, it's quite small.

But Gordon Creek did need a bridge. As it descends from Larch Mountain, Wahkeena (as it came to be known) produces a 240-foot double-tiered fall about 100 feet above the highway. The creek, reforming itself below, dances merrily down the twisted and bumpy hillside. It is one of the prettiest sights in the Gorge. The highway bridge Billner used here is a simple slab span. Later, the stone footbridge was added at the base of the falls.

The highway continues at an elevation just slightly higher than the Columbia River. Approaching Multnomah Falls, Lancaster and Billner

Mist Falls and basalt layers. *Photo by Dan Willis.*

Wahkeena Falls and the stone footbridge that Simon Benson had built after the completion of the highway. *Author's collection.*

were faced with the need for a couple viaducts. The tiny space between the railroad right of way and the side of the steep hill simply would not allow for a road. Because of the unstable slopes, removing part of the hillside was out of the question. Only by carrying the highway above the height of the trains—and slightly overlapping the right of way—were they able to take the road to and past Multnomah Falls. The west viaduct is 400 feet long, the east, 860 feet. Parts of the west viaduct rest on solid ground on the south side, but the east viaduct is freestanding along most of its length. Lancaster insisted on planting various flowering shrubs along the south side of the east viaduct, thus fooling travelers into believing they were still on solid ground.

The width of the two viaducts is seventeen feet, five inches—eight feet, eight inches per lane. Period. No shoulders, and no fudging. This width was adequate, of course, for early day traffic. Ford's Model T measured five feet, eight inches between the front hubcaps— the widest part of the auto.

Billner used a new style of railings for the two viaducts, repeating the arch theme but creating a lighter, airier impression and less actual

Multnomah Falls as God created it. *Author's collection.*

weight for the viaducts to support. The rock retaining walls needed to support the earlier style arched railings were not possible because of the thickness required at the base of such walls and the proximity of the railroad. In addition, these more solid-looking railings would have made the road width appear even narrower than it actually is.

The bridge crossing Multnomah Creek is a reinforced-concrete deck arch with solid spandrel walls. It might be described as "minimalist"—perfect for the overwhelming beauty of Multnomah Falls itself.

The upper fall plunges 542 feet to the pool below and then spills another 69 feet. The total drop is 620 feet, including the tilted, flowing surface of the pool between the two drops.

ONEONTA

Oneonta Gorge was one of the beauty spots Lancaster had selected as location points for the highway. Its two-hundred-foot walls—so close to each other they nearly seemed to touch—made the passage to the waterfall almost mystic. The two and a half miles of highway between Multnomah and Oneonta posed no real problems. Yes, the space was often narrow between the steep and delicate hillside and the railroad, but the road pushed through with only minor difficulties. But Oneonta Gorge was a different story. First of all, travelers at this point would not be able to view the waterfall from the highway, as it is tucked away, almost secretively, several hundred yards back in the gorge. That was a disappointment, of course, but those with

Oneonta Bluff. *Photo by Benjamin A. Gifford, courtesy of Old Oregon.*

a spirit of adventure could walk and wade (hip-deep) up the creek bed to view the falls. For the highway, there would be an eighty-foot bridge over Oneonta Creek, with railings echoing those on the Multnomah Viaducts. But just east of the bridge was an obstacle no road builder really wanted to deal with: Oneonta Bluff. This massive rock formation completely blocked the way.

A 125-foot tunnel was drilled, but not without difficulties. The rock was not as solid as it appeared, and workers had to inject cement into many cracks in order to stabilize the surrounding rock. The inside of the tunnel was also lined to prevent rock fall. The "overblast" space between the blasted hole and the tunnel lining was filled with cordwood. This tunnel was 17.75 feet wide and 17.5 feet high.

HORSETAIL

Just east of Oneonta lies Horsetail Falls. Aptly named, this waterfall appears to be plunging over the rump of a horse—that primitive means of travel before the advent of the thoroughly modern automobile. The railings for the sixty-foot bridge at Horsetail mimic the slab span at Oneonta and the Multnomah Viaducts. The highway at this point is so close to the waterfall that hot visitors could actually experience the cool spray as they drove by, a truly delightful experience.

Early day motorists often had to fix their machines no matter where, no matter what the weather. This photo is at Horsetail Falls. *Gifford photo, courtesy of Oregon State University.*

MCCORD AND MOFFETT

After passing Horsetail, the path of the highway was easy for several miles. There was enough land for the road, and no huge hills required that the road be extended in length.

The bridge at McCord Creek did the job it was designed for—carrying autos from one side of the creek to the other—but because of the lay of the land at the point where Lancaster chose to cross the creek, an extremely long bridge (365 feet) was required. It is utilitarian, but it doesn't have the arching beauty seen elsewhere along the highway.

In stark contrast, the bridge at Moffett Creek is one of the most beautiful in the nation. At 205 feet in total length, with a clear span of 170 feet, this bridge arch has a rise of only 17 feet. It was the longest, three-hinged, concrete flat-arch bridge in the United States at the time of its construction.

Constructing the roadbed for the McCord Creek Bridge. There must have been a special reason the family was allowed on the work site that day. *Courtesy of ODOT, Bridge Engineering section.*

Somehow, the beauty Lancaster and Billner loved is nowhere to be found on this bridge at McCord Creek. Beacon Rock is in the background on the Washington side of the river. *Courtesy of ODOT, Bridge Engineering section.*

The Moffet Creek Bridge more than made up for the lack of beauty at McCord Creek. The site is prepared for the pouring of the 170-foot arch in this photo. *Courtesy of the ODOT.*

91

The completed Moffett Creek Bridge. *Courtesy of ODOT.*

Although he was responsible for the bridge at McCord Creek, apparently Karl Billner was sidelined by the time of Moffett Creek Bridge's construction. The design is credited to Lewis Metzger. Charles Purcell was the engineer, and the contract for construction was awarded to A. Guthrie and Co. of St. Paul, Minnesota.

Tanner Creek, near the area called Bonneville, was crossed on a sixty-foot girder span.

Eagle Creek

After passing through several miles of land with adequate space for the construction of a road and with no problem avoiding the railroad's right of way, the highway again approached some tight places near the infamous Cascades area that was so troublesome to Oregon Trail immigrants. About

Above: Construction on the Toothrock viaduct. *Courtesy of ODOT, Bridge Engineering Section.*

Right: The Toothrock viaduct completed. *Photo by Ralph Eddy, courtesy of Clackamas County Historical Society.*

The Eagle's Nest, where travelers could stop and take in the view or even have a picnic. *Courtesy of David Sell.*

The Eagle Creek Bridge. *Courtesy of Friends of the Historic Columbia River Highway.*

two miles east of Moffett Creek is Eagle Creek. But it was impossible to get there, given the Highway Commission's restraints.

Once again, Lancaster designed a way past a seemingly insurmountable obstacle—at the location of the 1856 wagon road. "Toothrock," jutting skyward like an isolated canine tooth, was approached and bypassed by means of a viaduct. Immediately east of this tight passage, he designed an "Eagle's Nest," an arch railing–enclosed alcove alongside the highway where motorists could stop and enjoy the view or even have a picnic. There wasn't much space to pull an auto off the highway, but traffic in those days was light, so it was no problem.

A second viaduct east of Toothrock—the Eagle Creek Viaduct—is actually resting on a rock ledge for part of its width, making it a "half-viaduct." Just a little farther on, Purcell and Metzger built a bridge quite the opposite of the Moffett Creek Bridge with its beautiful low rise. The arch of the 103-foot Eagle Creek Bridge forms a half circle. It is constructed of reinforced concrete, which is seriously lacking in beauty, but is then faced with native stone, creating a wonderfully natural appearance.

THE MULTNOMAH COUNTY LINE

The Multnomah–Hood River County line crosses the highway just east of Eagle Creek. The highway through Multnomah County—from Troutdale to the Cascades—was completed, in time for the 1915 Panama Pacific International Exposition. It would be paved before the year was over and dedicated in June 1916.

15
HOOD RIVER COUNTY

CREST OF THE CASCADES

A s the highway continued east through Cascade Locks and into the town
of Hood River, it would cross a number of small creeks. Each of these
creeks has at least one waterfall associated with it; a few were easily viewed
from the highway.

At one time, a massive debris flow, the Bonneville Landslide, entirely
blocked the Columbia River. Eventually, the water overtopped the natural
dam, forcing its way to the sea. The natural land bridge—or more likely
the top of the dam that resulted from the landslide—came to be known as
the Bridge of the Gods. The rugged debris left behind caused the river to
tumble violently on its way to the sea, and this area—the narrowest part of
the Columbia River Gorge—came to be known as the Cascades, from which
the Cascade Mountains receive their name.

It was because of these rapids that the locks were built in the late 1800s.
But with the advent of trucks and automobiles, a good road was needed.

Hood River County—encompassing the crest of the Cascade
Mountains—stretches from just west of Cascade Locks to a point between
the towns of Hood River and Mosier, a distance of twenty-two miles. It is,
in some respects, the most difficult part of the Columbia River Highway,
challenging the engineers in ways they had not yet encountered.

And Hood River, with nowhere near the population of Portland, was
hard-pressed to raise money for something as extravagant as a highway.
Simon Benson stepped up to keep things moving. He promised that if the
Hood River County people would approve a $75,000 bond measure, he

As the workday is about to begin, these men show the primitive tools used in the monumental undertaking. *Author's collection.*

would pay for any overruns. And if that wasn't enough, once the measure was passed—by a three-to-one margin—he bought the entire bond issue within a month.

Various existing "roads" in Hood River County had grades as high as 18 percent. Despite negativism from many residents, on October 2, 1913, the county asked for a survey for the Columbia River Highway. The survey was begun on October 11 and was completed—all except the eastern section between Hood River and Mosier—by February 5.

While Samuel Lancaster had been the locating engineer for the Multnomah County section of the highway, his former student, John Elliot, was appointed (under Lancaster's supervision) to locate the road through Hood River and Wasco Counties. He began his work late in 1913, at the same time that things were getting underway in Multnomah County. This was a huge honor and responsibility for the young engineer.

John Arthur Elliott was born in 1884 in Cleveland, Ohio, the son of English immigrants. He received his AB degree from Willamette University in Salem, Oregon, in 1907 and his bachelor's degree in civil engineering from the University of Washington—where he studied under Lancaster—in 1909. He had held a number of engineering positions with various railroads and government departments, and Lancaster considered him equal to the job before him.

A very young John Arthur Elliott, photo taken about ten years before his involvement with the Columbia River Highway. *Courtesy of Oregon Historical Society.*

The newly surveyed road actually began in Multnomah County, and one mile of it was constructed by Simon Benson. It began just east of Eagle Creek, climbing a draw to put the highway a quarter of a mile back from the river, thus avoiding an unstable slide area.[47] It crossed Ruckle Creek on a tiny slab span and then meandered into the town of Cascade Locks and on toward two very difficult landforms. The highway designer was able to incorporate a county road for part of the distance. Continuing on, the highway pushed eastward and crossed Herman Creek on a one-hundred-foot girder span and Gorton Creek on a fifty-foot slab bridge.

The two major obstacles standing in the way of highway progress were Shellrock Mountain and Mitchell Point. It would take a great imagination and some pretty powerful engineering skills to overcome them.

SHELLROCK MOUNTAIN

Shellrock Mountain and Wind Mountain, twin talus slopes, lie deceptively still on the Columbia's shores, one south and one north. But these mountains hold a secret—soon discovered by the innocent victim who tries to traverse them. They are not still at all. They are on the move. Inch by inexorable inch, they continue to slide downward, although perhaps if we could leave them alone, that would not be the case.

Shellrock Mountain. Note the small remnant of the 1876 road in the lower left corner. *Photo by the author.*

In 1914, some portions of the 1876 road across Shellrock could still be seen (and can still be seen today), but the work done by prison labor in 1912 had, for all practical purposes, fallen victim to entropy.

Shellrock Mountain is now, and was at the time of the highway's construction, resting at an angle of about forty-two degrees. However, human activity—railroad/highway construction or quarrying—have encouraged the continual slippage of rock so that we can't trust the mountain to stay off the road.

Elliott's first job in traversing Shellrock Mountain was to remove the rubble that had once been the 1912 convict road. The retaining walls constructed by these "honor men" had been built with no understanding

A remnant of the old military road across Shellrock Mountain. *Photo by the author.*

Failed 1912 retaining wall attempted by convicts. *Courtesy of ODOT.*

The completed road at Shellrock. *Courtesy of ODOT.*

of the properties of rock and its ability—or lack of ability—to hold still: "Most of the walls seemed to have been constructed with the idea of making each rock go as far as it would."[48] The bottoms of the retaining walls were no thicker than the tops, with small, unfitted rock rubble behind them. No hammers were used to dress the rocks. The convict work actually increased the cost of the highway construction, as old, inadequate walls needed to be demolished before new, engineered walls could be placed.

The experienced stonemasons created an excellent wall along the lower edge of the mountain, just above the railroad tracks. They also lined the north side of the four-thousand-foot road with an arched railing like that used on much of the Multnomah County length of the highway.

Elliott had contracted with the railroad for a minimum clearance of 25 feet from the center of the track, with occasional exceptions of 16 or even 12 feet. No retaining wall was to be over 30 feet high. At tiny Lindsey Creek, Elliott requested that the railroad move its line to the north, since adequate land for this was available.[49] Understanding that highway traffic would ultimately be of benefit to the railroads, it complied, moving its tracks about 20 feet north for a distance of 1,800 feet. It was the only occasion when the railroad was moved for the highway—until the creation of the water-grade highway, years later.

The highway next crossed Lindsey, Wonder, Warren, Cabin, Starvation and Viento Creeks. Wonder and Cabin Creek were passed under the highway by culverts with masonry rock wing walls. Lindsey and Viento Creeks were crossed on eighteen-foot slab spans. The bridge at Warren Creek would be subjected to nature's abuse in its future.

MITCHELL POINT

Mitchell Point is composed of two erosional outcrops left after the great Missoula Floods. The lower feature, at 400 feet, is composed of Grand Ronde basalt. It has a notch in it, but this is not the "saddle." The big brother, at 1,100 feet, is capped by the Pomona Flow and underlain by Troutdale Formation river gravels. This gravel layer is more easily eroded and results in the 250-foot saddle between the two points. Through this saddle ran the telephone lines and the old state "road." This road, a part of the 1870s military road requiring nerves of steel to traverse, climbed at a dizzying angle over shale rock.

The newly married Ralph and Gladys Hinricks had quite an experience returning from their honeymoon, which Mrs. Hinricks related in this news story some years later:

> *Just at dark we got to Mitchell hill. The gas in our tin lizzy ran to the back of the tank and made going uphill most difficult. Ralph had to take the tent and everything off the car before starting up the grade. He drove that thing and I followed behind with a rock as large as I could carry. When the car stalled, I would shove that rock under a back wheel. Then he'd get it started up again, stall and I'd have to shove the rock again. Finally we got over the top and Ralph had to make trip after trip back down on foot to bring up all the things he had unloaded.*[50]

Interesting honeymoon!

This "road" continued toward Hood River over Ruthton Hill. The rocks in the area contained a phosphorescent mineral that made them glow in the weak light of the car lamps like the eyes of wild animals. Scary to say the least!

Profile of Mitchell Point showing Elliott's projected highway and the Little Boy Ranch house. *Courtesy of ODOT.*

It is no wonder the residents of Hood River were so excited about the Mitchell Point Tunnel. Well, after it was built, they were excited about it. Before, they had their doubts.

When John Elliott announced that he intended to put a tunnel through the lower point, opponents hired engineers to investigate. Their survey showed that the tunnel was not practical and that a better and less expensive road could be built through the saddle. The detractors' exaggerated interpretation of these "facts" was that the tunnel would be impossible to construct and that if it was started, it would never be finished.

Elliott's survey, on the other hand, showed that a road through the saddle would take a mile more of road, have poor alignment and heavy maintenance costs, and cost more than running a tunnel along the cliff face. He argued away his opponents' claims and invited bids.

Lancaster had seen a beautiful windowed tunnel in Switzerland. Elliott made Lancaster's dream his own. They would build the tunnel.

Elliott wrote of his work on the tunnel in his 1929 master's thesis for the University of Washington. Interestingly, he does not mention either Bowlby or Lancaster in his thesis. Lancaster, on the other hand, was quick to acknowledge Elliott's work on the tunnel.[51]

The greatest challenge was finding a place for construction that would not endanger the railroad below and would still be cost effective. Waste material at the bottom of the cliff could not come any closer to the middle of the track than twenty-five feet—although an exception had been made at Shellrock Mountain, where the buffer zone was reduced to sixteen feet. Presumably, Elliott could arrange for a similar easement here, but even then, it would be a tricky bit of work.

Elliott's locating party consisted of fifteen men: chief, draftsman, seven-man transit party, level man, level rodman, topographer, topographer rodman, tape man and cook. The cook was the most important member of the group, or at least, the one most appreciated by the others.

Great care was exercised in every aspect of the work, and much of the deskwork was done in the field, the paper fastened to a drawing board and covered with oilcloth for protection against the rain.

Elliott's reality check was this: "Any design, to be practicable, must be capable of execution at a minimum of expense and effort, using the accepted methods and equipment of the times."[52] In the end, his method cost less than a longer road over the saddle, took less time to complete and was doable within the confines of 1915 technology.

It was the best solution to the challenge of Mitchell Point.

BRIDGE AND VIADUCT

Piercing the heart of Lower Mitchell involved much more than just blasting a tunnel. The approaches at each end were a large part of the project as well, increasing the total length of the project to over eight-tenths of a mile.

The west approach, especially, was a challenge to Elliott's engineering skill, offering him the opportunity to try out just about everything he knew. As the road approached the cliff, projecting ribs had to be blasted away. A short bridge, resting partially on a rock shelf, was needed, followed by a 208-foot viaduct with an expansion joint.

In order to align the viaduct, men were let down over the cliff face on ropes 150 to 200 feet long to cut ledges in the rock for the placement of transits. Chaining—measuring exact distances with adjustable-length chains—was also done from the ropes, a most inconvenient position for such exacting work.

This west entrance constituted the greatest hazard of the entire job. The area being blasted lay directly above the railroad. For protection, the telegraph wires were taken down and buried in the railroad bed at the ends of the ties. Before each explosive detonation, the semaphore vanes were also taken down and the track protected by placing ties and logs alongside and over it.

Only small sections could be blasted at one time so the rubble could be removed before the next scheduled train passing.

After many days of wasted time firing one small shot after another and stopping in between to cover, uncover and clear the tracks, permission was granted to fire one large shot and pay the railroad to clear its own tracks with power equipment. The event was scheduled for Monday, May 10, at noon, immediately following the passage of the eastbound train. On May 9, the railroad moved in an extra gang in anticipation of the event.

The blasting went as planned. The cleanup did not. The maintenance engineer for the railroad, using both railroad employees and road workers, was supposed to have the tracks cleared by 6:00 p.m. Elliott noted in his report:

> *By the following morning twelve passenger trains and the fast mail were waiting in the vicinity of the Point, and freight trains were sidetracked for miles back...When the first train went by it was 47½ hours after the shot had been fired, and Mitchell Point had been put on the map.*[53]

Everywhere, the report was that Elliott had failed as expected, and the tunnel had collapsed, blocking the tracks. This gave the naysayers a thrilling but very temporary victory.

It was on this touchy section that the most serious injury of the Mitchell Point Tunnel work occurred. During a blast, the powder in one hole had failed to detonate. When a workman attempted to clean it out, the powder exploded, sending the poor man flying 140 feet away and dropping him in a rock pile. He was not killed, but as Elliott says, he was "badly broken up."

Once the rock ribs were taken care of, a half bridge was required. Half the width of the bridge was undercut in the face of the rock. The full width was twenty feet; it was only thirty feet long—short, but necessary.

Next came the 208-foot viaduct. The footings were four by four feet, except where there was no solid rock to set them on. Then, the size was increased to five by five feet. One crib for the pouring of support footings went sixty-five feet down with no sign of solid rock. Digging the holes was slow work by hand. Waste material was lifted from the holes by means of a hand windlass and then dumped down the hill and handled across the track below. Normal progress was three feet per eight-hour shift—pure drudgery.

Of the twelve footings required on the west viaduct, seven were seated on solid rock. The others were on (or rather in) shell rock.

PORTALS

The beginning of the Mitchell Point Tunnel. Notice the viaduct is not yet in place. *Courtesy of ODOT.*

While work progressed on the approaches, preparing the facings for the two portals was also begun. The first holes drilled were for the purpose of blasting a bench for the workers to stand on. Access was gained by the use of ladders and rope cages. In all, 6,100 cubic yards of material was removed to form the east portal and 226 cubic yards from the west.

When this was done, a small tunnel was driven along the centerline. It was six feet square and timbered. A track was built into the tunnel and a one-yard car used on the track. The car ran out to the dump location, and a horse was used to pull it back. Before long, the horse had learned the routine and would return to the dump, turn around and wait patiently to pull the car back into the tunnel. Four men and the horse could remove as much as two hundred cubic yards of rock in a day.

By mid-July, the tunnel was being moved forward at a rate of about three feet per shift, and the first window opening was begun. Entrance was still gained by a series of ladders, since the viaduct was not yet in place.

THE TUNNEL ITSELF

The width of the tunnel was to be eighteen feet, with no shoulders. The sides would be ten feet high, with a nine-foot radius arch above.

In Switzerland's Axenstrasse, the pillars between the windows are built up of masonry rather than being a native part of the rock from which the tunnel was cut, and the tunnel is considerably shorter than the one at Mitchell Point. Elliott felt he could do better. He intended for his tunnel, including the outer, windowed wall, to be entirely hewn from the rock cliff. To do this, required a safe exterior wall thickness. It couldn't be too great or the windows would look more like tunnels leading off to the side. The ceiling thickness also had to be adequate.

Elliott was criticized at first for putting a curve in the tunnel. But he felt it showed the windows to greater advantage and allowed them to better light the interior of the tunnel. Later his critics agreed with him. And of course, cutting the windows was exacting work. Elliott wrote:

> First the weak places, the indentations in the cliff, were spotted on the map as cheap window locations. A minimum wall thickness of eight feet was next spotted on the map…After considerable testing and trying of the sections, five windows were located, which were considered sufficient to adequately light the bore…The windows were grouped as one, three, one, and were 16 feet wide by 19 feet high…At the fifth window a trail was laid out for 25 feet along the cliff [utilizing extra and unwanted thickness of the wall at that point]. From this trail could be seen the face of the cliff where the windows were out, and an excellent view up and down the river would be obtained.[54]

Driving the tunnel began at the west end but soon was progressing toward the center from both ends. Once the opening at the west end of the tunnel had progressed beyond the first window location, the window opening was started and work progressed more slowly. Extreme care was taken on this part of the project. Too little explosive was preferable to too much. Total length of the bore was 390 feet. The two ends met on July 13, 1915.

On July 17, 1915, a number of Portland's most influential citizens were escorted on a tour from Portland to see the tunnel, still under construction. After a very early but sumptuous breakfast[55] hosted by Amos Benson, the group motored eastward, stopping at a number of the most awe-inspiring sites, and arrived at Mitchell Point in midafternoon. In addition to Benson, the party included Lancaster and Bowlby and a number of highway promoters. The purpose of the trip was to build support.

Originally, the design had called for window openings with natural rock benches. But at the first window (the westernmost one), Elliott found it was impossible to get the top of the railing smooth enough, and he changed his mind. The natural bench was removed, and railings of rubble and concrete masonry were installed.

In order to ensure extreme care in the driving of the tunnel, the contract placed a premium on close work. A variation of 5 percent from the specified section was allowed without any adjustment in price. For overbreak between 5 and 10 percent of specified section, the contractor would be paid at a lesser rate, but if the overbreak exceeded 10 percent, no allowance would be made.[56]

Upon completion of the bore, measurements were taken using a special device designed for the purpose. When the first seventy-five feet at the west end of the tunnel produced no variation greater than 5 percent, the bid price was accepted.

CONCRETE

The concrete plant was located on a platform just outside the railroad clearance line near the west end of the project. The cement house was at one end of the plant, the mixer and hoisting engine in the middle and the other end was reserved for sand storage. Some of the rock from the tunnel was used as coarse aggregate.

Concrete was mixed on the platform, put into a half-yard bucket, hoisted up to the grade above, dumped into cars and run along the track to the viaduct. Water for the concrete, lumber for forms and the reinforcing steel also had to be hoisted up from below. The plant had to be shut down whenever a train passed—a nuisance to say the least. Progress was tedious.

Pouring of the deck was begun at the east end of the viaduct and extended to the expansion joint, 128 feet west. The continuous pour took thirty-nine hours. The west end was poured six days later in a brisk eighteen hours. The concrete was spaded and tamped by hand and cured under a 3-foot layer of dirt.

Surprisingly, the tunnel itself was not the most expensive part of the job. The tunnel, including the windows, rails and trail, cost $37.10 per linear foot. The viaduct cost $41.10 per linear foot.

The exterior of the Mitchell Point Tunnel at the left, with the viaduct, center, and the "half-bridge," right. *Brubaker Aerial Surveys.*

East portal of the Mitchell Point Tunnel from a postcard lithograph. *Author's collection.*

Bids were opened on St. Patrick's Day, March 17, 1915. Work began only two weeks later, on March 31. The road opened to traffic on September 6—less than six months later—and was completed on November 10. An amazing timetable, especially considering the construction methods of the day.

RUTHTON POINT AND HOOD RIVER

With Mitchell Point Tunnel in the rearview mirror, Ruthton Point was the next obstacle to overcome. This massive formation would have been too expensive to climb over or blast, so Elliott chose to go around it. The difficulty did not compare with Mitchell Point or Shellrock, but it required careful planning and hard work. And he took care to avoid the need for railroad crossings, which, on the old county road, were at grade and very dangerous.

Once east of the point, the way to Hood River (the town) was clear. The highway passed through town on Cascade Avenue and Oak Street. Lewis Metzger designed the 420-foot bridge across Hood River (the river) in 1918 to replace an old timber bridge.

Ruthton Point as it appears today. The Columbia River Highway (center left) swung around the point. Today's Interstate 84 plows right through it. *Courtesy of Friends of the Historic Columbia River Highway.*

LEAVING HOOD RIVER COUNTY BEHIND

Once again, adequate space along the bank of the river was not available. Elliott did consider running a line on the south side of the tracks, as it would have been the shortest route. But this would have required extensive grading. He also considered following the general path of an existing county road but found that it would need to be more than twice the length of the lower route and would climb to almost 1,600 feet before descending to Mosier— only a little higher than Hood River. Elliott sought a route between the two extremes. But he resigned before anything was finalized.

In the end, it was Roy A. Klein, Elliott's replacement, who designed the last bit of highway in Hood River County. In October 1917, he suggested yet another possibility for a road between Hood River and Mosier.

Klein's highway would climb to a summit of only 530 feet, eliminating much of the distance that would have been required to bring Elliott's higher-elevation road into compliance with the 5 percent grade restriction. The new proposed route was only a little over six miles. Granted, it rose steeply at first. Klein created the Hood River Loops, very similar to the Figure Eight Loops near Latourell, to handle the problem.

The highway crested just east of the county line. And not too far past that, the final obstacle to the highway's forward progress stood stubbornly in the way.

16

WASCO COUNTY

SUNSHINE AND DRY AIR

B y late 1916, Elliott was hired as the highway engineer for Wasco County, but he focused his attention on other county roads while Klein took charge of the Columbia River Highway. The highway's momentum was slowing considerably. Work was progressing well on the westernmost length of the highway—from Astoria to Portland—but to the east, many Wasco County residents felt no urgency to tax themselves for the purpose of replacing "perfectly good" roads with newfangled improvements. Roy Klein intended to replace them anyway.

MOSIER TWIN TUNNELS

While the work was still mainly accomplished with hand tools, a few machines were beginning to appear on the scene. The earliest segments of the highway had been constructed entirely by hand, with the help of horses. But by this point, steam shovels and air drills were brought in to help with some of the heavy work. Still, it was a challenge.

In 1920, work was begun on the twin tunnels. Right from the start, these tunnels, and the cliff of which they are a part, had demonstrated bad behavior, throwing rocks down on the unsuspecting. But there just seemed to be no other way—or at least no better way—to get the highway from Hood River to Mosier, in Wasco County.

West portal of the Mosier Twin Tunnels, showing observation points outside the tunnel. These are reached through openings in the side of the tunnel. *Photo by Arthur Prentiss, collection of Alonso Robisco (Spain).*

Klein's plan was to blast a few of the smaller obstacles—basalt ribs jutting into the path of the proposed highway—and tunnel through the two largest barriers. The west tunnel was short—only 81 feet—followed by a 24-foot open space and then by the longer eastern tunnel, at 288 feet. This longer tunnel curved slightly and had two "adits." These adits, or short side tunnels, led to windows overlooking the river and the Bingen Anticline on the Washington side—a beautiful view of this massive geological formation. One of the adits led to an outside stairway and "cliffwalk" for an even more open view.

The boring of the tunnels was completed by July, the work having been at least partially financed through Oregon's new gas tax—the first in the nation.

Emerging from the east tunnel, the change between the land west of the Cascade Mountains and that to the east seemed complete. Where before the hills had been covered with Douglas fir, maple, ferns and mosses, now the land appeared much more open. The vegetation was primarily pine and scrub oak, trees that thrive in drier climates. This was also a land of poison oak and rattlesnakes—"amenities" not found on the west side of the mountains. Undergrowth, if it existed at all, was minimal.

The average annual rainfall in Troutdale is forty-seven inches, as it is in Corbett and Bridal Veil. By Eagle Creek, this amount increases to sixty inches, and Cascade Locks tops the charts at over seventy-six inches of precipitation per year. By Hood River (only twenty miles east), the wet stuff has been reduced to less than half, at about thirty-two inches, and by The Dalles, it is a mere fifteen inches. So it is no wonder the vegetation changes so dramatically.

Through this progressively drier climate, the highway descends without further difficulty from nearly four hundred feet at the tunnels to a little over one hundred feet in the village of Mosier.

Rowena Crest

Exiting Mosier, the highway crosses the 1920 Mosier Creek Bridge. In appearance, it is somewhat similar to the bridge at Shepperd's Dell, but this 182-foot arch span was designed by Conde B. McCullough, Oregon State bridge engineer from 1919 to 1935. A beautiful waterfall on Mosier Creek is not visible from the highway but is only a short walk away.

The highway climbs gracefully through scabland very similar to that left in eastern Washington by the ice age floods. This area, at six to seven hundred feet in elevation, experienced the same incredible scouring power as is seen along most of the Columbia River below Grand Coulee.

This land and climate produce masses of beautiful wildflowers through the spring, summer and fall. Lancaster's highway continued to be a place to revel in the beauty of Creation, even after emerging from the tight constraints of the Gorge itself.

Parts of the new highway in this area follow older county roads. Dry Canyon, near the summit of Rowena Heights, required a bridge, even though there was no water nearby. McCullough designed a smaller version of his Mosier Creek Bridge—101 feet as opposed to 182 feet—and set it in the small, steep canyon in 1921.

At Rowena Heights, almost immediately beyond the bridge, a high table of land waited, just begging to be made into a View Point along the highway. Larger than Thor's Heights, this location presented no particular engineering challenge, and a loop road and parking area were provided for

Rowena Crest and the upper end of the Rowena Loops. *National Archives.*

Aerial view of the Rowena Loops. *Courtesy of ODOT.*

115

the travelers' enjoyment. But just beyond the summit lay another opportunity for Lancaster's now famous loops. J.H. Scott located the road down from the heights. His line did not incorporate the parallels seen at Latourell or Hood River, but the graceful, curving road could be viewed, nearly in its fullness, from the top as it descended to the village of Rowena—the staging area where Oregon Trail pioneers had loaded their possessions and themselves onto rafts for the last leg of the journey.

After descending from the heights, the highway followed an abandoned railroad alignment about ten miles into the town of The Dalles.

At the western edge of The Dalles, the highway crosses Chenoweth Creek on a 1920 McCullough girder bridge—the formal end of the Gorge portion of the Columbia River Highway.

17

PAVING THE HIGHWAY

R avenel's *Road Primer for Children* was published in 1912. This 150-page textbook, intended for use in schools, covers every aspect of road building, including basic mathematical and engineering skills. Building good roads was, to the children of the early 1900s, what computer literacy is to their school peers one hundred years later—everyone should understand and be able to apply the knowledge.

And through the children, and the push to create good roads for automobile traffic, adults everywhere were jumping on the bandwagon. Public sentiment began to shift from, "The old roads are good enough" to, "How can we make this even better than we imagined?"

Paving was not something new in the early twentieth century. Road engineers in Europe had been working on various methods of hard-surfacing roads since at least the mid-1700s—not to mention the even earlier roads of cobblestones or brick.

Around 1820, a Scottish road engineer came up with a new method for hard-surfacing roads. John Macadam became the commissioner of paving in Bristol, England, in 1816, one hundred years before the construction of the Columbia River Highway. In his work on the 149 miles of road for which he was responsible, he discovered that roads need not be constructed of massive amounts of gravel, as had been done in the past, but that a good layer of gravel on a stable surface that was covered with a road "crust" to protect the soil underneath from water made an excellent road. The three courses of gravel he laid, in decreasing sizes, were broken by hand (with small hammers), the top layer being smallest. These top stones needed to be smaller than the width of a carriage (iron) tire. The action of the tires on the gravel would gradually cement the small stones together with their own dust. This method worked very well for iron tires. It is the method Lancaster had used in Jackson, Tennessee.

Unfortunately, roads constructed in this way were not appropriate for the rubber tires of automobiles. It was an awkward time—the teenage years of road surfacing. Lancaster's work, especially at Maryhill, had produced volumes of information concerning materials, temperature at which the compound should be laid, methods of application and aftercare of the surface.

But it would cost money. Fortunately, Multnomah County citizens had fallen in love with their new highway and, after the expected back-and-forth discussions concerning value versus cost, voted in 1914 to tax themselves for road improvements. They spent $900,000 to improve and pave the Baseline Road as it led from the heart of Portland out to the Sandy River.[57]

They next proposed paving the section from the Troutdale Bridge to the Stark Street Bridge and, then, all the way to the county line. The Warren Company won the contract in June 1915 and had the work completed by October that year.

Gravel was made on site as needed by this rock crusher. *Courtesy of Troutdale Historical Society.*

The paving material they used was called Warrenite. The mixture, which included crushed rock and a form of oil or tar, was prepared in a "batch plant" and was called "hot stuff" by the workers.

Rock crushers were used to provide crushed rock of assorted sizes. Crushers were moved as needed to decrease the amount of rock to be hauled. And accompanying the crusher, a batch plant was put in place at each location. The hot stuff was spread two inches thick by hand and compressed by mechanical roller.

On June 27, 1922, Simon Benson ceremoniously spread the last shovelful of paving material over the roadway near Rowena. With this, the Columbia River Highway (later designated Highway 30) was officially completed from Astoria, at the mouth of the Columbia River, to The Dalles.

18

NOT ALL SWEETNESS AND LIGHT

H enry Bowlby was fired. John Elliott quit. Sam Lancaster walked away. And "Johnny" Yeon, that amazing roadmaster who was liked and respected by pretty much everyone, blew up.

As with any project of this magnitude—and especially in uncharted waters—politics played its part. Apparently Bowlby had the audacity to insist that contractors not be paid until they finished their job according to the contract specifications. And he felt they should be paid only what had been promised. Some people felt otherwise. On January 12, 1915, James Withycombe replaced Os West as Oregon's governor. By February, state highway engineer Bowlby's resignation was requested.

> *By formal resolution the State Highway Commission this morning requested the immediate resignation of Major H.L. Bowlby as State Highway Engineer. It is understood that in case the engineer refuses to resign, his official decapitation will follow forthwith. The resolution calling for the resignation was conveyed by telephone to Major Bowlby by George P. Putnam the private secretary of Governor Withycombe, a few minutes after the board ended its brief session, about 11:30 o'clock.*[58]

It was made clear at the session that the legislators had no faith in either Bowlby's competence or his executive ability and that "if the commission did not remove Bowlby, there would be no road legislation at this session, and affairs [would] be left in a tangle for the next two years."[59]

The charges related to a thirty-eight-mile section of road in Hood River County and included that "a large wall had fallen, the road was narrow in places, the bridges had been built insecurely, the line had been changed…and what was a good macadamized road in many places had been torn up until nothing but a mire of mud remains."[60]

"Personally," said Governor Withycombe, "I have the highest regard for him and believe that he is a much misunderstood man, but…" And so, Bowlby resigned. He announced he was ready to turn over the office of state engineer as soon as his successor was sent to take charge of it.[61]

The *Journal* called it "one of the greatest scandals in the political history of Oregon."[62] But Bowlby wasn't the only one.

Elliott found himself in hot water also. The March 6, 1915 *Morning Oregonian* reported that Governor Withycombe had "taken under advisement" a controversy concerning John Elliott, who was being accused of "meddling, incompetency, and even moral lapses."[63] These charges apparently stemmed from increasing tensions between Elliott and the Newport Land and Construction Company of Hermiston, which had won the bid for construction. Elliott insisted that only Italians be employed as stonemasons; the company wanted to hire Greeks for half the cost. Elliott wanted to fire certain workers he felt were incompetent; the company said they were just fine. And then, just to liven things up, Elliott and Ross Newport (owner of the company) had a fistfight! Elliott's nose was broken, and he sued the company for $10,000. Newport was quoted as saying Elliott was "devoid of all principles of justice and without the milk of human kindness."[64]

Upon completion of the Mitchell Point Tunnel, Elliott decided he'd had enough. He took the highway past the challenging Ruthton Point and into Hood River and then resigned to work on other roads in Wasco County and leave the rest of the Columbia River Highway to someone else. Roy Klein replaced him.

Samuel Lancaster also ran into trouble when Lightner and Holman, concerned about overrun costs, refused to sign his vouchers for salary. By April 1915, with the highway in Multnomah County almost finished, he resigned. His engineering work on the highway was essentially complete, and the little work that remained was finished under John Yeon's supervision and according to Lancaster's detailed instructions.

Herbert Nunn took over for Lancaster during the last couple months of the work in Multnomah County. But he worked *under* John Yeon. Then, in 1917, Nunn stepped up as Bowlby's replacement, when Oregon's Highway Commission was restructured.

The highway had cost more than predicted. The paving had cost more than predicted. And Vista House (which will be covered in the next chapter) was costing way more than predicted. The patience of the commissioners was wearing thin, as was John Yeon's. At the October 10, 1917 county commissioners' meeting, when Holman objected to Yeon's suggestion that the road near Shepperd's Dell needed to be straightened, the meeting got very interesting. The *Oregon Journal* reported that Yeon said to Holman, "You are a damn big booby!"[65] Yeon suggested someone go for the sheriff, "but no one left their seats, not wanting to miss anything."[66]

Considering all the things that could possibly go wrong and all the personalities involved, perhaps it truly is a miracle road—a miracle that it was ever completed!

PART 4

WHAT CAME AFTER

VISTA HOUSE

O nce the highway through Multnomah County was essentially complete, things continued happening fast. Retail establishments for the sale of gasoline and repair of tires and engines were needed immediately, and they sprang up like seeds in fertile soil. Simon Benson bought up large parcels of land around Multnomah and Wahkeena Falls and gave it all to the City of Portland for public use. While the road's promoters still billed it, at least partly, as a farm-to-market road, it was, indeed, the well-to-do automobile owners who took to the road in ever-increasing numbers. And these auto enthusiasts wanted not just the necessities but also the niceties—places to dine and possibly lodge overnight, as well as places to stop for ice cream or a hot dog.

By far the most spectacular tourist facility along the new highway (and one of the most spectacular in the nation) was Vista House. With the highway completed to the county line, the auto owners of Multnomah County were ecstatic. They began driving not just to get from one place to another but also for relaxation and entertainment. But it wasn't long before the ladies began to notice a profound lack of "comfort stations" along the new road. Perhaps typical of men, they hadn't worried too much about such niceties during the construction phase, nature providing all they needed in the way of sanitary facilities. But the women were distinctly unimpressed with such "natural" answers to their needs. They wanted bathrooms, nice clean bathrooms with flushing toilets and sinks where they could wash up.

Not to worry, assured their menfolk. A proper facility would be constructed as soon as possible.

Celebration at Crown Point on June 6, 1916. President Woodrow Wilson unfurled the flag by the touch of a button in Washington, D.C. *Courtesy of Alex Blendl.*

On June 6, 1916, two dedication ceremonies were held for the Multnomah County segment of the Columbia River Highway. The first was at Multnomah Falls, the second, later in the day, at what was now called Crown Point (Thor's Heights). At this second ceremony, President Woodrow Wilson, unable to attend the celebration in person, participated by touching an electric button in Washington, D.C., which unfurled an American flag at the dedication site. The groundbreaking ceremony for Vista House took place at the conclusion of the dedication.

The original budget, approved by the Multnomah County Board of Commissioners, with the encouragement of Julius Meier, was for $17,230. Renowned architect Edgar M. Lazarus was hired to design the structure. The original plans called for a modest building constructed of concrete and wood, with stucco on the exterior and interior walls of plaster.

The Vista House Association was formed for the purpose of raising the needed funds. Henry Pittock was named president. He and the other forty-eight influential Portland businessmen who made up the association were to raise $9,000, which would be matched by Multnomah County.

In the beginning, auto owners were encouraged to pledge five dollars each to the construction of the comfort station. Next, a weeklong campaign targeted churches, women's clubs, schoolchildren, pioneer families (whose ancestors would be honored in some concrete way in the new building), businessmen and employers. Even with all this frenzied activity, the money raised was not what the promoters had hoped. The Vista House Association had managed to raise only $4,000, less than half the amount it had hoped for. Julius Meier, believing strongly in the project, talked the county commissioners into contributing $12,000, and construction began.

While Lazarus was the architect, Lancaster gave considerable input to the interior design, and Roadmaster John Yeon continued to serve as supervisor without pay.

Construction began in September, but it was a false start. In November, Commissioner Rufus Holman raised questions and complained of irregularities in the plans for Vista House. By this time, the original estimate of less than $18,000 had mushroomed to $30,000 and then $50,000. Holman, one of the original supporters of the construction, had the good sense to point out that the proverbial emperor was naked. Or rather, the coffers were empty. Contractors, worried by the talk of not enough money, stopped their work fearing they would not be paid.

The public outcry was two pronged. Supporters wanted whatever Lazarus, Lancaster and Yeon produced. The opposition wanted fiscal responsibility. Work finally resumed in late December when Holman, in spite of his pronounced reservations, voted along with the other commissioners to accept—and fund—the changes.

One year into the construction, the $50,000 was consumed and the taxpayers of Multnomah County were asked to bear the burden of yet another $15,000.

Rufus Holman stated, "Our nation is at war…Our national government must have first consideration, and our local government must therefore curtail its program accordingly." He felt that spending such a huge sum on a "toilet facility" was "an outrage on the confidence of the public."[67] Holman was the hinge upon which swung the two opposing forces. He stood tall, said what he considered to be the truth and refused to back off. The board of commissioners continued to vote, albeit reluctantly, to allocate funds as needed.

Unfortunately, at least for the taxpayers who eventually were strapped with the bill for $100,000, Lazarus, Lancaster and Yeon were all men of deeply artistic nature who believed anything could be done. So little by little, they expanded on the design and purpose of Vista House, much to the dismay of those whose feet were more firmly planted in the realities of wartime.

A lawsuit, perhaps backed by Holman, was brought in 1918 by an enraged taxpayer. Nora Withrow sued the county commissioners, the Vista House Association and everyone else she could think of—even Lorens Lund, who had donated the property on which the building stood—charging "breach of trust, fraud, deceit and misrepresentation." By the time of the hearing, eleven more names were included with Withrow's. All of them, including Withrow, admitted they had never seen the petition before signing it. The defense held that the commissioners did, indeed, have the authority to build Vista House. It was considered "an emergency measure in the interest of public health and sanitation." The suit was dismissed.[68]

Work was finished on May 1, 1918. The total cost was $99,148.05, almost six times the original estimate. But Vista House stands today, a monument not only to Oregon pioneers but also to the dreamers who insisted on moving forward even in the face of strong and reasonable opposition. Practicality says they should have backed off. But the many travelers from around the world who visit disagree. Expressions such as "Marvelous!" "Amazing!" and "What a view—nothing like it in the world!" fill the visitors' books.

Much of the work on Vista House was done by the same hardworking men who had labored to construct the highway. The Italian stonemasons did the masonry surrounding the building and some of the building itself. At least one of them, Mr. Camillo, used the same stone that faces Vista House for the exterior of his own home in a predominantly Italian neighborhood in Portland.

But it wasn't only Italians who were involved.

FRANK ACKERMAN: MARBLE CUTTER

Marion Ackerman Beals tells of her father's involvement in the Vista House:

My father, Frank Ackerman, was born in Milwaukee, Wisconsin, in 1874. His father was a titled gentleman from Germany, who, on arriving in the United States, left his title at the immigration desk, proudly declaring that titles had no part in his new life in America. His young bride, Louisa, was a Lafayette from France—the Lafayettes who helped in the American Revolution.

Marble Setters, during my father's time, were paid in gold coin. My older brother, John, would receive a gift of a five-dollar gold piece each Christmas.

The uniform of the trade was white canvas pants, a suit coat and a hat to match. Father carried a matching heavy canvas bag, with leather trim, that contained his tools. There were polished tombstones in our basement, awaiting names and inscriptions.

One time, I watched my father chisel an inscription marked only with chalked lines and spaces for words, all carefully measured. But the lettering was done by a perfectly held chisel and with a few taps of his mallet. At Vista House, he created the limestone drinking fountains.[69]

The basement of the building was constructed first, of course, followed by the stairs leading up to the future observation deck. No building surrounding them—just two stairways jutting skyward. But the building soon followed. It included the main floor rotunda, a basement that housed two very nice restrooms and the caretaker's quarters and an observation deck surrounding the upper level of the rotunda.

The aboveground part of the building is forty-four feet in diameter and fifty-five feet high, while the lower level is sixty-five feet in diameter. The floor of the rotunda, the stairs treads and bathroom stall dividers are Tokeen Alaskan Marble furnished by the Vermont Marble Company. The inside walls (including their hand-carved

Frank Ackerman, master marble carver, aboard the *Bailey Gatzert*, one of the best-known steamers on the Columbia. *Courtesy of Marion Ackerman Beals.*

Hand-carved limestone drinking fountain in the Vista House rotunda. *Photo by Dan Willis.*

Crown Point and the beginning of the Vista House construction. The highway begins its descent toward Latourell even as it circles the point. The basement is structurally complete. Notice that the stairs leading to the upper observation deck are in place before the exterior of the building was constructed. *Courtesy of Troutdale Historical Society.*

The rotunda's reinforced concrete exterior and roof are nearly complete in this image. One of the stairways can be seen through a large window opening. *Morrison Electric Company photo, author's collection.*

drinking fountains) are primarily Kasota limestone from Minnesota, with a few parts composed of plaster or plaster-of-Paris. The dome and ribs are painted to simulate the marble and bronze originally planned. Apparently, a few of the grand ideas proposed were set aside in the face of the ongoing conflict over funding.

The eight plaster-of-Paris Native American busts adorning the upper portion of the rotunda depict four men—each looking across the rotunda at a mirror image of himself. Plants native to Oregon adorn the frieze panels just above and between the Indian heads: chestnut, oak acorns, pine cones, grape, apple, wheat, Oregon grape (the state flower) and ginkgo. These panels also display the names of eight prominent Oregon pioneers: Dr. John McLoughlin, James Nesmith, Joseph Lane, Ashel Bush, Jesse Applegate, Matthew Deady, Reverend Jason Lee and Marcus Whitman.[70] The colored windows of the upper level and part of the

main level are "opalized" glass. The viewing area, of course, has clear glass. The exterior of the building is of light gray Tenino sandstone (mounted over reinforced concrete), and the roof is of green glazed tile.

The Vista House was completed on May 1, 1918, and dedicated on May 5. Rufus Holman, when asked to deliver the dedication address, refused and was absent from the festivities.

Spectacular as it is, even the impact of Crown Point's view is surpassed by the powerful forces of nature. The east wind at Crown Point has often been clocked at well over one hundred miles per hour. Three "life time guaranteed" flagpoles had to be replaced before the company that sold

Lorens Lund (and canine companion) standing beside the stone-clad Vista House. It was Lund who donated Thor's Heights for this modern miracle. *Courtesy of Tony Jones.*

them finally caught on and dropped the lifetime warranty. Now, the flagpole is removed each winter and replaced in the spring.

Over the years, Vista House itself has also suffered the effects of both wind and water. Leaks developed everywhere, encouraged by the freeze-

This iconic photo of Vista House at Crown Point was taken from Chanticleer, looking east. Beacon Rock is in the distance. *Courtesy of David Sell.*

thaw cycle and the winds. The sidewalk prism glass, pumping daylight into the lower level, also leaked and was repaired, and leaked and was repaired, and so on.

In 1982, the Friends of Vista House formed to try to rescue the broken beauty. Stopgap measures helped a little, but eventually, the Friends and the Parks Department closed down the structure in 2000 for a major restoration. Now that the building was listed on the National Register of Historic Places, policies were in place to assure that any restoration would only rehabilitate the building, not change it. This added constraint caused the restoration bill to top $4 million. But it also ensured the historic integrity of this masterpiece so treasured by people from all over the globe.

A hydraulic lift, invisible except when in use, is now in place, allowing mobility-impaired visitors access to the lower level—a privilege long denied them. This feature would appeal greatly to Sam Lancaster, that lover of beauty, who was a survivor of paralyzing polio.

The story of Vista House and Crown Point could have had a far different ending. By January 1916, ninety-six lots were platted atop Crown Point, with the expectation that they would be filled with homes belonging to people who could afford to live in this spectacular setting:

Logged off Crown Point was platted as "Thor's Heights," a series of lots beckoned to builders of coffee shops and service stations along the new Columbia River Highway.

In 1915, Richard T. Dabney announced plans for a massive hotel to wrap around Crown Point. A gondola would lift tourists from Rooster Rock Station on the railroad to his Tudor Gothic building. The hotel's giant pipe organ and chimes would broadcast concerts through the Gorge for miles.

Dabney died in 1916 and with him, the hopes of a hotel, gondola and pipe organ evaporated. Only the twinkling street lights of Crown Point remind later generations of what might have been.[71]

20

SIGNS AND LINES

Louise Ports, a talented artist from Springdale, just east of Corbett, hand-painted and lettered the original highway signs from Troutdale to the Hood River County line. And once they were up, she could often be seen in good weather perched on a ladder, restoring, by hand, the signs along the highway.

Peter Rexford of the Multnomah County Sheriff's Department is the man who thought up the centerline (at least in Oregon, if not in the nation) as a way for vehicles to stay safely on their own side of the road on dark, rainy nights. After a particularly harrowing nighttime bus ride in the pouring rain, Rexford came up with what he thought was a good solution. Remembering the white line his father had marked on the ground at the family farm leading across a ravine to the bunkhouse, Rexford suggested a similar line for the Columbia River Highway. When the county declined to fund the stripe, Rexford bought the paint out of his own pocket.[72]

As with the early road building, much of the associated work was done by locals. When Rexford provided paint in 1917, Frank Knieriem and Dave Butler, Corbett-area farmers, painted the center stripe from the Summit to Latourell by hand. A short time later, a line was painted inside the Twin Tunnels.

Sometime between Rexford's innovative striping of the highway and 1954, the centerline color had changed to yellow. By 1958, the U.S. Bureau of Public Roads mandated white. The outcome of ignoring this mandate would be the loss of $300 million or more in federal funds for improvements to U.S. 99 and U.S. 30 (Columbia River Highway). Oregon capitulated.

But after only two years, the yellow lines were back—at least on the state highways. Oregonians just preferred yellow. After all, on a road covered with snow, yellow will show through long before white!

Currently (2014) all U.S. highways and freeways use yellow to separate lanes going opposite directions and white to separate lanes traveling in the same direction. Sounds like Oregon had it right all along.

21

OTHER ROADHOUSES IN THE GORGE

The first roadhouse along the Columbia River Highway was, of course, Chanticleer Inn, which had been there since 1912, before the highway was begun. By 1914, Margaret Henderson had decided to part ways with Mr. and Mrs. Morgan and open her own restaurant at Latourell Falls.

Latourell Falls Chalet opened to the public in October of that year and was an immediate success. "Here one may find such food and shelter as he perhaps has dreamed of but has seldom experienced," boast hyperbolized travel guides of the day. The building was just to the east of this magnificent 225-foot waterfall and on the south side of the highway. Tragically, it burned only three months after opening. The roadhouse—including a "grand piano, phonograph, tapestries, paintings, silverware, and a year's supply of her beloved jam"—was a total loss.[73]

Chin high and optimism intact, Henderson purchased land and began construction of her third roadhouse in a most auspicious location—overlooking Crown Point. She called it the Crown Point Chalet. The new inn opened with a "house-warming" party in the middle of May 1915. Short on cash for building, Margaret sold twenty-dollar "dinner books" (to be redeemed later) to a number of Portland businessmen, who were more than happy to have a part in the recovery effort.[74]

The Crown Point Chalet opened on May 15, 1915. It had an indoor garage on the lowest level, the restaurant above it and sleeping quarters for Henderson and the girls who worked for her on the top floor. Margaret's father, H.L. Darling, did much of the interior woodwork in the chalet. In

Margaret Henderson's Crown Point Chalet, with Vista House in the background. *Courtesy of David Sell.*

December 1915, it lost its roof in one of those famous Gorge east winds, but it was soon repaired.

The inn thrived into the late 1920s, registering in its guestbook many local travelers as well as the wealthy, the famous and dignitaries from America and around the world. Names such as Fritz Kreisler, Frank W. Woolworth, Roscoe "Fatty" Arbuckle, Count Ilya Tolstoy, Ronald Colman, Charles Chaplin, Henry Ford and Queen Marie of Rumania are recorded in the books.[75] One of the most frequent guests was John B. Yeon, the highway's roadmaster.

Chanticleer Inn was destroyed by a fire in 1930. It might not have happened had Margaret Henderson still been in charge of operations. She stoutly refused to serve alcohol at her restaurants, knowing that drivers under the influence of alcohol would be unsafe. The Chanticleer fire is thought to have started when an intoxicated guest left a cigarette in a bathroom wastebasket.

Gardiner's Café opened in 1922 and was originally called Johnson Confectionary. It was located next to Vista House on the east side of the highway and served the public until 1963, when it was torn down by the U.S. Forest Service.

The Multnomah Hazelwood was an ice cream and refreshment stand located at Multnomah Falls from 1916 until 1919, when it was torn down. Its ice cream came from the Hazelwood Creamery in Portland. The Union Depot Station was connected to the ice cream shop for part of this time. From 1919 until 1925, when the Multnomah Falls Lodge was built, visitors could drive their automobiles or ride the train from Portland but would have to bring their own refreshments for the trip to magnificent Multnomah Falls.

Multnomah Falls Lodge was designed by renowned Portland architect Albert E. Doyle, who is also responsible for the Meier and Frank building and the Benson Hotel. The lodge is designed in the Cascadian style and is made of stone and timber. Every type of rock found in the Columbia River Gorge is represented in the building.

The lodge was dedicated in 1925, with the restaurant under the management of Rolla Simmons, who also owned a restaurant in Portland. He called his new business "Simmons-by-the-Falls." He remained manager there until November 1942, when the restaurant was closed for the duration of World War II. It reopened in February 1946 under a new manager. The ownership of the lodge was transferred to the U.S. Forest Service in 1939, and today, it is operated by the Multnomah Falls Company.

Multnomah Falls Lodge has undergone several overhauls and upgrades with additions over the years. It was enlarged in 1927, 1950, 1960 and 1994. It currently offers an interpretive center, restrooms, a gift shop, a snack bar and a lovely restaurant with a view of the falls. It does not, however, offer "lodging," in spite of its name.

Maffett's Villa, also known as Latourell Villa or Falls Villa, was built in 1916 just across the highway from the location of Margaret Henderson's short-lived Latourell Falls Chalet. Here, a traveler could find lunches, confections, cigars or a soda. Owner Harold Maffet decided to improve the view of the falls from his establishment and arranged to blast the hillside where Latourell Falls Chalet had been with high-pressure water, in an attempt to eliminate it. He was unsuccessful, but he did manage to produce a mudslide of some magnitude, which flowed down Latourell Creek to the boat landing on the river. Larger boats were no longer able to dock, and Maffet's name became "Mud!" The Villa was torn down in 1959.

Forest Hall, a classic Colonial-style building on the north side of the highway between Shepperd's Dell and Bridal Veil, was built in 1915 as one of the many roadhouses along the Columbia River Highway. It has, for some time, functioned as a private residence.

Bridal Veil Lodge was opened in 1927 as an eatery, lodge and auto camp. There was also a nearby garage for the benefit of auto travelers.

For $1.50, a carful of intrepid adventurers could pitch a tent in this lovely location, perhaps after enjoying a hearty dinner for $0.50 apiece. Or for those who preferred a bit more luxurious accommodations, rooms in the lodge or in one of several small cabins were available.

The building is constructed in a rustic style from locally harvested timbers sawn at the Bridal Veil mill. The lodge closed in the mid-1940s, but in 1987, it was reopened by a descendant of the original owners and converted to a bed-and-breakfast.

View Point Inn opened in June 1925 and was originally known as the Palmer House. It is located on land once owned by Lorens Lund—a part of the same 120-acre tract that encompasses Crown Point. Its point of entrance, however, is Larch Mountain Road. The View Point Inn is on the other side of the rise from Crown Point Chalet and Vista House.

The property was purchased from Lund by Mrs. Grace Palmer, who hired a Portland architect to design and build a Tudor arts-and-crafts style "teahouse and resort." It opened to the public on June 4, 1925.

Forced into bankruptcy in 1927, Mrs. Palmer sold the business to William Moessner, highly respected chef at Portland's Benson Hotel. Moessner renamed the house View Point Inn, and he and his wife, Clara, ran the business for over fifty years, entertaining some of the same notables as Margaret Henderson.

As traffic was gradually rerouted to the water-grade highway, the View Point Inn found itself with fewer and fewer customers. Moessner, however, remained ready to serve should a tourist happen by. He died in 1979, still tending his empty inn, and the property was purchased by Doug and Karen Watson, who assisted in getting it placed on the National Register of Historic Places in 1985. The Watsons did not operate the house as an eatery, choosing instead to live in it as a home.

The house changed hands again in 1997 but, since that time, has had an unfortunate history. On Sunday, July 10, 2011, the historic beauty suffered near fatal burns. A spark from a chimney ignited a three-alarm fire. The entire top floor was gutted, and the cedar shake roof destroyed. It was left unprotected through the following winter and beyond. Restore Oregon, an organization seeking to preserve Oregon's past, placed the building on its official list of "Oregon's Most Endangered Places" in 2012.

Multnomah Lodge was constructed in 1916 at the base of Mist Falls. It was often called Mist Lodge to avoid confusion, although Multnomah *Falls* Lodge was not constructed until 1925, nine years after the opening of Multnomah Lodge. This eatery served both dinners and light lunches at moderate prices and offered overnight accommodations also. It was located halfway between Portland and Hood River, being thirty-five miles from each of them.

A severe winter storm in 1921 nearly spelled the end of this fine establishment when the heavy snow accumulation caved-in the roof. The

Multnomah Lodge below Mist Falls. *Courtesy of David Sell.*

The fireplace, now decked in moss, still stands on the location of Multnomah Lodge at the base of Mist Falls. The lodge burned to the ground in 1929. *Photo by Dan Willis.*

owners, however, rebuilt, and the lodge continued to function until it was destroyed by fire in 1929. The fireplace, now covered with a blanket of moss, is still standing just off the south side of the Columbia River Highway.

Lindsey Inn, located on Lindsey Creek between Shellrock Mountain and Mitchell Point, was the location of another roadhouse that served tourists. In addition to meals, one could get soft drinks, cigars, new tires or gasoline here.

The Little Boy Ranch at Mitchell Point, built by the Parker family in 1912, became another rest stop along the Columbia River Highway in the early 1930s, when the house and property were purchased by Elsie "Babe" Tenny. The Parkers had unknowingly created a perfect house to serve as a rest stop, with two huge fireplaces in the main room and a glass-enclosed veranda. In addition, the location offered a wonderful view and was very close to the famed Tunnel of Many Vistas.

Mrs. Tenny, with her two young sons, abandoned the Dust Bowl in Oklahoma and Texas and moved to the lush, green Columbia River Gorge in search of a better life. True, the Little Boy Ranch was on the drier side of the Cascade Range, but still, it was quite an improvement over a land that kept blowing away by the truckloads.

Babe converted the ranch house to a sandwich shop. She also sold fuel and built a dozen or so cabins to lodge weary travelers. The coffee pot was always on, dances were a regular occurrence and Babe very thoughtfully provided dry travelers with enough moonshine to keep them happy—until her still was confiscated by the authorities. The building no longer stands.

The property went through several owners until, in 1960, it was donated to the Oregon State Parks by the Vinzenz Lausmann family. Today, it is the location of the Mitchell Point Overlook, just west of the former location of the viaduct. It also serves as the trailhead for two hiking trails.

The Columbia Gorge Hotel was built by Simon Benson in 1920. This was just at the time business could be expected to increase exponentially, and Benson knew what to do about it. He created a place where tourists could not only rest from their journey but also find pleasure and even opulence. The footbridge over Phelps Creek and the short walking path through the grounds were created to mirror the lovely rockwork of the highway. Wah-Gwin-Gwin Falls tumbles over a cliff near the building. As he had done with his Benson Hotel in Portland, he planned for his establishment to serve as a model, setting a high standard. He said:

My main thought is not a profit-making enterprise, but to express my ideas
of what a tourist hotel ought to be as an adjunct to highway development and

tourist attraction. It is not only essential to make our valleys and mountains accessible by good highways, but it is further necessary to capitalize them by pleasant and comfortable hotels.[76]

From the start, the Columbia Gorge Hotel was known as a place of luxury. It had a dining room measuring forty by seventy-six feet and forty-eight rooms, each with a private bath. It was patronized, in its heyday, by the likes of Jane Powell, Myrna Loy, Rudolph Valentino and even two presidents—Roosevelt and Coolidge.

During the Depression and war years, the hotel lost business and gradually became run-down. It was purchased in 1952 by the Neighbors of Woodcraft and converted to a retirement home. By 1978, the hotel's future was looking bright once again as corporate owners began a $1 million restoration. It reopened in September 1979 and has been serving as both an elegant restaurant and fine hotel since that time. The grounds have also been restored to their former glory. The hotel was closed briefly in 2009 but was reopened and sold to a Pendleton hotelier. Condominium units have been added in the original style.

Highway Maintenance and Evolution

Footbridges at Multnomah and Wahkeena

Multnomah Falls, by its very configuration, almost demands a footbridge. In fact, a wooden bridge existed at the site in 1885 but was lost prior to the highway's construction. In a letter to Billner on July 16, 1914, Lancaster said he had given Mr. Benson the plans and requested specifications for construction of the bridge.[77]

Billner responded from Bridal Veil on August 9, enclosing the completed plans, and said that both sides of the bridge site were cleared of brush and that the points of the bridge were set

The wooden footbridge between the two tiers of Multnomah Falls, 1885. *Author's collection.*

Multnomah Falls with the Benson footbridge. *National Archives.*

on bedrock.[78] Both this bridge and the one at Wahkeena were completed shortly after the highway's dedication.

The Benson Bridge, as it is called, was especially difficult to construct considering its location. The use of machines and animals was out of the question in the rugged terrain. An aerial trolley was put in place to lift construction materials to the site, and the bridge was constructed without falsework.

THE GREAT SNOW AND ICE STORM OF *1921*

The weather in the Columbia River Gorge in 1921 was dreadful. The east wind, never a gentle force, blew with a fervor unknown for many years, and the sky dropped snow and frozen rain without mercy. Troutdale was sealed in ice. The entire Gorge was frozen stiff.

Traffic of all kinds screeched to a halt in November of that year. Samuel Lancaster and other lovers of the highway were appalled that nature would be so cruel. Many locations along the length of the road needed remedial attention when spring finally came. It was found that the effects of the ice were so severe that Multnomah's east viaduct had been seriously damaged and needed considerable restoration. It was upgraded with improved strength in the support system.

The highway was drifted completely closed in a number of places. Two travelers were stuck in the eastern tunnel above Mosier and left a memento of their ordeal in the form of a rock carving. It reads:

SNOWBOUND
NOVEMBER 19 TO 27, 1921
CHAS T. SADILEK
E.B. MARVIN

Presumably the work on this "historic graffiti," or at least the ending date, was done the following spring. Once they were able to escape, they probably didn't wait around to carve rock.

By the time the storm abated, massive amounts of white stuff blocked the entire 250-mile distance between Walla Walla, Washington, and Portland. In some areas, it was more than fifty-four inches deep. Some drifts in the Gorge were as much as twenty feet deep.

ABOUT GRAVITY

The balance between nature and man has always been a tenuous one. Man "conquers" nature, pats himself on the back and then—sometimes when least expected—nature kicks up a fuss, nullifying man's proudest accomplishments.

The section of road for which Mario Cerighino gave his life has been a problem ever since its construction. The cliff-side road slips and slides slowly down the hill only to be shored up again every few years. In 2006, the southwestern end of this section was reinforced with gabion baskets—metal baskets filled with rock—and has held well since that time. But there's still a section that needs attention every couple years or so. The new paving material added to bring the road surface back up to grade builds up year after year. Well over twenty feet of accumulated surface material was brought up by a recent core sample.

Rockslides have been an ongoing problem with the highway. After all, the very thing that makes this area so beautiful also makes it likely to surrender to the force of gravity. In addition to the rocks tossed down randomly near the various tunnels, occasionally rocks that have fallen during the night will be discovered by a morning driver on the highway.

This rock was dragged to the parking lot at Vista House after it fell to the road nearby. *Photo by the author.*

In February 1918, a massive debris flow near St. Peter's Dome (east of Horsetail Falls) covered the highway for a distance of five hundred feet at a depth of ten or twelve feet. Some of the boulders in the slide weighed as much as ten tons.[79] While this section of the highway had been constructed by men with shovels, once the road was actually in place, it was possible to bring in a steam shovel to remove all this debris.

On September 4, 1995, Multnomah Falls performed its most notable feat in known history when a chunk of rock the size of a school bus (and weighing as much as that bus filled with cement) detached from the wall behind the falls and fell to the splash pool below the Benson Bridge.

Multnomah Falls sees upwards of 2 million visitors each year, and September is one of the busiest months for tourists. Even so, no lives were lost, and the injuries were minor and few—most of those injured being members of a wedding party posing for pictures on the Benson Bridge, an unforgettable wedding memory!

Record rainfall in February 1996, following close on the heels of an extended period of below-freezing temperatures, caused a massive debris flow south of the Hersh and Carol Royce home between Horsetail Falls and Bonneville. The mud, rock and trees smashed into the back of the home,

Replacement dry masonry wall near Shepperd's Dell under construction. *Photo by the author.*

filling the main floor up to the kitchen counter tops. Both the Royces and their horses in the field outside made their way to safety, but the home was a total loss and has never been rebuilt.

On January 9, 2014, the Benson Bridge took a major blow from a falling boulder. Portions of the deck and railing were broken off. The bridge and the trail beyond it will remain closed until repairs can be made. Only a few days later, on January 12, a rock the size of a Volkswagen fell onto the eastbound lanes of I-84 near Hood River. Fortunately, no injuries resulted from either event.

Much of the stonework seen along the Historic Columbia River Highway is original—built mostly by those talented Italian stonemasons—but some of it is new. Sometimes the new is hard to tell from the old, as moss grows quickly in this area, especially west of the Cascade crest. Just as each master mason one hundred years ago had his own unique style, today's masons often express their individuality in their work. Traveling the Historic Highway is not only an adventure back in time but also a stroll through an art museum. A person could spend a lifetime soaking in the beauty of this area—both natural and man-made.

THE "NAIL PICKER"

During the 1920s, Roy Klein, state highway engineer and designer of the Wasco County section of the highway, took note of the many vehicles stopped along the highway for the repair of flat tires. In this day before the introduction of steel-belted radial tires, it was all too common a sight. Klein heard of a student at Washington State College who had mounted a large, powerful magnet underneath a truck for the purpose of picking up nails and other metal objects along the highway. The machine was commonly referred to as a "nail picker." Those old autos could shake loose an amazing number of nuts and bolts as they chugged down the road. Klein decided to try the machine on Oregon roads, and in 1928, records showed that it was picking up thousands of pounds of junk, which, in turn, cut the number of flat tires noticeably.

ONEONTA TUNNEL

The tunnel at Oneonta Gorge was bypassed when the railroad track was moved north onto fill land in 1948. The highway was moved northward, slipping between the bluff and the railroad tracks. The tunnel was backfilled.

In 2006, as a part of the ongoing "Remember, Restore, Reconnect" effort of the Friends of the Historic Columbia River Highway and the Oregon Department of Transportation, the tunnel was reopened. The U.S. Forest Service and Federal Highway Administration were also part of the project. Unfortunately delays ensued, but finally, in 2009, the tunnel was completed, lined for safety and opened for use. It is now a part of the Historic Columbia River Highway State Trail.

McCORD AND MOFFETT BRIDGES

The McCord Creek Bridge was used, with some upgrades, as Interstate 84 westbound until 1997, when it was replaced. The Moffett Creek Bridge was bypassed but has recently been added to the Historic Columbia River Highway State Trail.

BONNEVILLE DAM

Sam Jackson had begun suggesting—even promoting—a dam on the Columbia River as early as 1891. And his was only one of the voices heard on this subject. At the time of the construction of the Columbia River Highway, the river still ran free. The thundering falls of Celilo, the amazing "river turned on its side" at The Dalles, and the frightening rapids of Cascade Locks were very much a part of the highway experience. The views of the river from the various view points along the highway's length revealed a frothing, leaping, dancing cataract rather than the series of still lakes we see today.

But then, progress happened. In the wake of the Great Depression, the country was actively looking for ways to put men to work and, at the same time, improve the quality of life for all Americans. A dam would be a good thing, they said. It would produce electricity and prevent floods,

Bonneville Dam. *Courtesy of Troutdale Historical Society.*

and its locks would allow much easier passage of boats, opening the way for greater commercial interaction with the interior: eastern Oregon and Washington.

The site was selected and construction on the dam, the first in a ten-dam project, was begun in 1934. It was determined that both the railroad and the highway would need to be relocated. In addition, a campground that Sam Lancaster had created near Bonneville[80] had to be blasted out of existence to make a place for the dam's powerhouse. Lancaster, even though his Camp Get-A-Way had been precious to him, fully supported the construction of the dam and, in 1935, designed and laid out Bonneville Park for use by government and construction workers.

The dam is one of the largest on the Columbia River. It, along with other dams in the project, is computer controlled from Vancouver, Washington.

TOOTHROCK TUNNEL

The part of the highway requiring relocation at the time the dam was built was the Toothrock section, between Moffett Creek and Eagle Creek. It was decided that a tunnel should be constructed through the formation atop which the viaduct sat. It was the first tunnel in the nation to have interior electric lights.

Beginning the Bonneville (Toothrock) Tunnel in 1936. *Courtesy of David Sell.*

The Bonneville Tunnel (west portal) at the time of its construction. *Courtesy of David Sell.*

Bonneville Tunnel (east portal) after lowering the roadbed to allow for higher-profile vehicles. *National Archives.*

Eventually, this new tunnel was incorporated into Interstate 84. While the westbound lanes ran north of the tunnel, the eastbound lanes plunged through it, a bit intimidating at sixty-five miles per hour—especially since the tunnel has a curve in it. In preparing the tunnel for freeway use, the roadbed was lowered three feet (in effect, raising the ceiling height) to allow for higher-profile trucks. It is also sometimes called the Bonneville Tunnel.

While the original highway at Toothrock is no longer open to vehicular traffic, hikers and bikers today can still travel this section and even pause to look down on the freeway traffic entering or exiting the tunnel below. The trail passes over the restored/repaired Toothrock and Eagle Creek Viaducts.

THE WATER-GRADE HIGHWAY

The Columbia River Highway was on the path toward obsolescence almost before it was finished. Motor vehicle traffic grew both larger and faster more quickly than the highway's designers had ever imagined. The first section of the water-grade highway put into use was between Bonneville and Cascade Locks at the time of the dam's construction. By the 1950s, the water-level route was complete, just in time for work to begin on a modern freeway, which incorporated much of the water-grade highway. Each of these new roads was straighter and had less elevation change than its predecessor.

EAGLE CREEK BRIDGE

Eagle Creek is less than a mile upriver from Bonneville Dam. Bonneville Lake backs up nearly to The Dalles, so obviously, Eagle Creek is affected. The water level has been raised, but also, as the creek's water flows more gently, it no longer has the power to roll rocks and boulders out of the way. So gradually, the bed of the creek has risen as well.

Eagle Creek has long been one of the foremost salmon spawning grounds in the Northwest. A hatchery has been established here (and one at Bonneville also) to aid the salmon. It's man's attempt to overcome his folly—or lack of foresight—in building a dam across a living river. That balance between progress and preservation is sometimes very hard to find.

Eagle Creek Bridge after the construction of Bonneville Dam raised the water level. Compare the height of the arch to the photo on the bottom of page 94. *National Archives.*

Bridge of the Gods

The man-made, delightfully airy Bridge of the Gods (constructed in 1926 at ninety-one feet above the river level) served auto and truck traffic well until the gates of Bonneville Dam were closed in 1937. Because the lake forming behind the dam would raise the level of the river, the bridge would also have to be raised to allow large boats to pass under it. In 1938 through '40, the bridge was raised forty-four feet and had to be lengthened as well to accommodate the wider river.

And yes, Charles Lindberg flew his Spirit of St. Louis under the bridge in September 1927.

Shellrock Mountain

After the construction of the new highway around the base of Shellrock Mountain, the hillside kept sliding. And it is sliding still.

A sheltered remnant of the original highway just east of Shellrock Mountain. *Photo by the author.*

In spite of this, some portions of the 1876 road, as if defying nature, are still in existence. The freeway today is protected by a sturdy half-mile strip of retaining wall (a "bin wall" topped by a Brugg fence) as it rounds the base of the slippery hill. Just behind the barrier lie the remains of the Historic Columbia River Highway. Another section can be seen just east of the Shellrock segment.

MITCHELL POINT TUNNEL

In the beginning, the hard-hearted practical types had rejected the idea of a tunnel through Mitchell Point. But once their hearts were softened, they fell in love with it. They were proud of it. They wanted all the world to come see this amazing blend of God's beauty and man's ingenuity. And people came to see it and marvel. The people of the Gorge, and especially Hood River, almost popped their buttons.

But just as time and the success of the tunnel had changed their hearts in 1915, by 1939, change was again campaigning for the hearts of men, and they yielded. At least, many of them did.

The location of the former Mitchell Point Tunnel showing the huge gash where the viaduct crossed and the roadbed on both sides leading to the tunnel. *Photo by Dan Willis.*

They had good reason. The tunnel was not behaving itself. It seemed to be growing narrower by the day, as the size of cars and trucks grew. Meanwhile, the mountain continued tossing rocks on unsuspecting visitors, and at one point, it produced a rockslide that covered the tunnel's west entrance and closed the railroad for a time.

By 1939, insecure rock near one of the windows was causing concern for railroad officials. One of the pilasters was reinforced with concrete, and the window next to it was closed. Still, rock continued to fall. With the increased size and speed of motor vehicles, traffic lights were installed, limiting traffic to one way at a time. Engineers made detailed studies, and it was decided the safest thing to do would be to move the railroad north onto a bed constructed of fill material in the river. They closed the tunnel and constructed a new water-level road between the Mitchell Point cliff and the river. This water-level highway was under construction at various places along the length of the Columbia River Highway, and Mitchell Point was just one more section in this effort.

In December 1954, R.H. Baldock, state highway engineer, wrote that the Mitchell Point Tunnel "should never be reopened, because of the danger to the people using the road, and an official would certainly assume a grave responsibility if he knowingly permitted traffic to be subjected to the positive danger involved."[81]

Traffic was diverted to the as-yet-unfinished water-grade highway, the railroad track having been moved already into the river. In 1954, the tunnel was closed and backfilled. Twelve years later, it was blasted away to widen the roadbed for Interstate 80 (now I-84) and provide fill for its construction.

It was one of those polarizing events that wrench the hearts of men. Some were glad to see it go. Some said it was a travesty. But the fact is it's gone, a victim of progress.

Oregon Department of Transportation, Oregon Parks and Recreation Department, The Historic Columbia River Highway Advisory Committee and the Friends of the Historic Columbia River Highway are planning to reconnect all remaining segments of the highway from Troutdale to Dalles.

HOLE-IN-THE-WALL FALLS

Meanwhile, as if the difficulties of constructing a road around Shellrock and through Mitchell Point weren't enough, the area between the two began to cause problems. It was the issue of road maintenance. As all road engineers

Hole-in-the-Wall Falls (Warren Creek Falls). *Courtesy of Michael Pike.*

know, water is the enemy of good roads. But in this case, the water was causing a slightly different kind of problem.

Warren Falls, at ninety-six feet, tumbled over a cliff of columnar basalt similar to that at Latourell Falls. It was beautiful. But it would occasionally store up rocks, logs and other debris at the top and then, during a high-water event, fling them, without remorse, over the edge to threaten the highway and railroad bridges below. The highway bridge had been repaired several times, but something more permanent needed to be done. The problem must be fixed at its origin, decided the highway department. Several options were discussed, and the final decision was to divert the falls. A tunnel was blasted through an adjacent cliff and a huge iron grate placed across the opening. This was the birth of Hole-in-the-Wall Falls. The plan also mandated a new (and very ordinary) highway bridge to replace the poor beaten and battered bridge that had been damaged so many times.

The new bridge was built in 1939 and functioned pretty well as long as it was needed. Eventually, the old highway gave way to Interstate 84, located farther away from the bottom of the cliff. But Hole-in-the-Wall Falls is still there, in all its "glory." It is, however, only a matter of time until something will need to be done. The iron grate and the weir at the tunnel entrance are showing their age, but with a bit of ingenuity, it would be entirely possible to divert the water back to its original course and reestablish Warren Falls.

THE MOSIER TWIN TUNNELS

These tunnels were narrow (as were all the tunnels on the highway). One-way traffic lights had been installed, but eastbound vehicles, when stopped, became sitting ducks for the rocks tumbling down near the west portal. Not surprisingly, people objected. The rockslides became almost constant, and finally, traffic was diverted to the unfinished water-grade highway below while the tunnels were backfilled. In 2000, the tunnels were reopened to the public as a part of the Historic Columbia River Highway State Trail. It is accessible to antique motorized vehicles three to five times each year and serves as a hiking/biking trail the rest of the time. A "rock catchment" was constructed between the two tunnels (twenty-four feet) and at the west end (seven hundred feet) to protect visitors from rock fall, which continues to this day. These catchments look a bit like some of the viaducts originally constructed for the highway, but people travel under rather than over them.

The roof is made of foam, pea gravel and a compacting concrete that can absorb the energy of a five-thousand-pound boulder falling two hundred feet. Some people think it is ugly, and perhaps it is. But it's safe.

ROWENA LOOPS

It has been discovered that meandering, looping roads are good for more than just reducing grade in mountainous areas. They can also be used for commercials showing how well a particular make of auto can handle corners. The Rowena Loops as well as the Maryhill Loops have been used in this way.

And both these areas have been used for antique auto drives. Auto buffs from all over the Northwest—and sometimes even farther away—come to show off their machines, exchange information, enjoy each other's company and motor through this unique wonderland in the tradition of a slower, more peaceful time. Those who really want to get into the spirit of the adventure even dress in period clothing.

ONGOING MAINTENANCE

Many highway structures and the road itself have been revitalized in recent years using modern technology while maintaining the original purpose and character of the aging beauty.

In one example, the Horsetail Creek Bridge, in October 1998, received a well-deserved upgrade. The civil engineers who tackled the project used "fiber reinforced polymers," one of the new substances in structural engineering.[82] The appearance of the bridge is unchanged, but its youth is renewed.

In the case of the historic white rail fences, the new replacement fences are steel backed and have been crash-tested at fifty miles per hour. The traditional white rail fences are still used on the hiking/biking portions of the state trail.

The highway continues to receive needed maintenance through the Oregon Department of Transportation.

WHAT HAPPENED TO THE PEOPLE?

MARGARET HENDERSON

One of the great things about Sam Hill was his habit of affirming others. He wrote this letter to Margaret Henderson on June 9, 1927:

> *Dear Mrs. Henderson,*
>
> *Having recently read the long list of the names of the men who admit that they each severally and alone built the Columbia River Highway it occurred to me that even at this late day as I have not yet written anything on the subject I should like to add a name to the list, that of one who modestly has made no claim to being the constructor of the Highway. I mean Margaret E Henderson who shared with each and every one the hardships of the pioneer work and who when the laborers returned at night foot sore and weary cheered them with excellent meals—who which [sic] they slept in beds which she had provided—rose and built the fires, and prepared hot and appetizing breakfasts and may I add that without these kind attentions the road might never have been built. May I then as an old and admiring friend add this tribute.*
>
> *Your friend*
> *Samuel Hill*[83]

Although Margaret Henderson's Crown Point Chalet was valued at $78,000 in 1925 (a good-sized amount in those days), she was not always at the top of the business world. Struggling with health issues, Margaret sold the chalet in 1927 and opened a small third-floor dining room in Portland. Finally, failing health and the effects of the Great Depression forced her into bankruptcy. She lived the rest of her years in Portland and died at the age of fifty-eight in 1930. Her obituary, typical of the time, noted not only her great success in promoting the construction of the Columbia River Highway and her reputation as an excellent restaurateur but also the fact that she "died penniless"—an unnecessary bit of information, to say the least, especially considering the number of penniless people during the Depression.

JULIUS MEIER

Julius Meier, president of the Meier and Frank Company, lived at the Benson Hotel in the winter months and at his estate, Menucha, in the Columbia River Gorge during the summers. The estate is between Corbett and Chanticleer (now called the Portland Women's Forum State Park). It currently belongs to the Presbyterian Church and is used as a conference/retreat center.

Meier was elected governor of Oregon in 1930. During his term, the Oregon State Police was organized. He chose not to run again in 1934 because of health concerns and died at Menucha on July 14, 1937.

SAM JACKSON

The *Journal*, under Sam Jackson, became the state's largest evening newspaper, and his reputation as an excellent journalist extended across the nation. In 1917, Jackson donated eighty-eight acres of land as a park in Portland. It is now the campus of Oregon Health Sciences University (OHSU). He died in 1924.

HENRY PITTOCK

After many years of repeatedly mortgaging his home to pay the *Oregonian*'s debts, finally, in 1909, Henry Pittock began planning a lovely twenty-two-room mansion for himself and his wife. The Renaissance Revival mansion sat on forty-six acres of woodland—quite a switch from the tiny house in the city. It was completed in 1914, when Henry and his wife were eighty and sixty-eight years of age, respectively. It was listed on the National Register of Historic Places in 1974, and tours are available there. He died in 1919.

HENRY BOWLBY

Henry Bowlby consistently referred to himself as "Major Henry L. Bowlby." Apparently, the man had no lack of self-esteem. And despite the fact that no one else knew it by that name, he referred to the Mitchell Point Tunnel as "the Bowlby Tunnel" in an article he wrote for *American Forestry* in 1916.[84]

JOHN YEON

"Johnny" Yeon was remembered fondly by workers on the highway and residents of the Gorge for many years. His personality and work ethic were such that people just liked the man and would work hard for him. In addition to his work on Vista House, in 1917 and 1918, he was a supervisor of the Spruce Division for Oregon, involved in providing spruce for the construction of airplanes to be used in the war. In 1919, he somewhat reluctantly accepted the position of head of the State Highway Commission under Governor Ben Olcott. His first responsibility was to direct the expenditure of the monies collected under Oregon's new gas tax.

John Yeon died in October 1928 at the age of sixty-three.

SIMON BENSON

Benson had a deep and abiding love of learning and a great admiration for the benefits of a good education. He saw the need for a school that would teach young men how to work. Eventually, he provided money to establish Benson Polytechnic High School in Portland.

The school concentrates on the teaching of many technical arts and applied sciences. The new lamps for the Crown Point viaduct were made there.

Benson agreed with Stewart H. Holbrook, writer for the *Oregonian*, who wrote, "Many able housewives, plumbers, and electricians have been ruined by Greek and Latin piped into them in their early lives."[85] Benson's daughter, Alice, quotes him as saying:

> *The reason I gave $100,000 toward establishing the Benson Polytechnic School was to give our boys a chance to learn trades and become self-supporting, self-respecting citizens. If a man has a trade, he can earn money. This means that he is apt to get married and own a home. The forces of discontent can make no converts among workmen who own homes and have family ties. We need fewer men who are looking for white-collar jobs. I have no interest in a man who is unwilling to sweat.*[86]

Benson, in spite of being one of society's leaders, was not at home in "society." He was his own man, the kind of man who makes a much better leader than follower and who isn't interested in what people think of him. He just did what he did and was who he was.

Alice Benson Allen remembered this about her father:

> *He had a good sense of humor and was fun to be with. One time, in response to a question about his family background he* [said], *"Never mind me; we were farmers and originally pirates."*[87]

He eventually retired to Los Angeles and died there a month short of his ninety-first birthday.

SAM HILL

In 1914, Hill began laying the groundwork for his "castle" on the north bank of the Columbia. He had purchased seven thousand acres on the bluff above the wide Columbia some time before with the express purpose of developing a model home and town. Never mind that a town already existed on the site. Columbus, as the town was known then, was changed to suit Hill's plans. Soon, he had built a church, roads and a dam and named "his" town Maryhill. The residents took it in stride.

Hill's plans for his "home" at Maryhill were as huge as everything else in his life. He referred to this building as "a good, comfortable and substantial farmhouse." But by 1917, he had stopped construction.

His friend Loie Fuller, the dancer, suggested he make it into an art museum. Finally, in 1926, when it was somewhat finished, he invited Queen Marie of Rumania to come to America and dedicate the house as a museum. She obliged and brought along several "royal" items, which she donated to Sam's infant collection of art and artifacts.

The greatest disappointment in Sam Hill's life was his lack of an heir. Try as he might, he was unable to prod his son James into a sense of responsibility on this subject. And his daughter, suffering as she was with schizophrenia, never married. So he had children, but they were not "worthy" heirs of his good name and fortune.

But then, his son Sam B. Hill was born to Mona Bell, one of Hill's several mistresses. Sam had arranged a marriage between Mona and his cousin, Edgar Hill, thus legitimizing the child's birth and giving him the Hill name. There were two other children as well, born to two different mothers.

Hill built a mansion near Bonneville, adjacent to Sam Lancaster's Camp Get-A-Way, for Mona. It was a beautiful place, and the broken foundations and nonnative plants brought in to beautify it can still be seen there. When Bonneville Dam was under construction, Mona was requested to relinquish ownership and move out. She objected, and a court case ensued. After being awarded a fair price for the house and land by no fewer than two juries, she still was unable to fight the U.S. Army Corps of Engineers successfully. She didn't want the money. She wanted her house. She was finally evicted in May 1935, when her son was almost seven years old. The mansion was divided into two apartments—one downstairs, one up—and was used by the Corps, at least intermittently, for housing.

Sam Hill, upon his death in 1931, left money for the care of his daughter, Mary, whom he loved deeply. He also left a monthly allowance to his wife and their son. In addition, he left larger amounts of money to the three other women who bore him children and to the children themselves.

Sam Hill, who was never accused of minimizing his accomplishments, took credit for making Henry Ford and John D. Rockefeller two of the richest men in the country. Without Hill's roads, Ford's cars would not have sold well. And without Ford's cars, Rockefeller would have had no use for his petroleum.[88]

Just as the highway through Multnomah County was nearing completion, the *Oregonian* reported that Sam's years of public benevolence were coming to an end. According to the story in the paper, Hill said, "I have been a soldier for good roads since July 1, 1875, and now, after 40 years of toil and tribulation, I am determined to step aside and allow someone younger, stronger and richer than myself to carry the good work on."[89]

In 1915, Sam built what may have been the first monument to peace in celebration of the peace existing between the United States and Canada for the previous one hundred years. It is a massive arch located on the Canadian border near Blaine, Washington.

In 1918, he built a full-sized replica of Stonehenge as a memorial to Klickitat County[90] soldiers who had died in the war. When asked to explain why, he said, "Because I wanted to remind my fellow men of the incredible folly of still sacrificing human life to the god of war."[91]

Sam Hill died in 1931 and is buried just below Stonehenge in the Klickitat hills of Washington State.

SAMUEL LANCASTER

When the county commissioners refused to pay Lancaster in 1915, he left Portland to supervise roadwork at Rainier National Park. John Yeon paid Lancaster's back wages out of his own pocket.

In the ensuing years, Lancaster designed roads and parks at Linfield College, Bryce Canyon, the Grand Canyon and a number of other places.

He also wrote *The Columbia: America's Great Highway*, extolling the beauty of the road.[92] He took many of the photographs that appear in the books himself. He wrote, "While going back and forth over the Columbia River Highway during its construction I carried my camera in a rain-proof bag in all kinds of weather, that I might be ready when God painted the pictures."[93]

In 1922, Lancaster purchased a seventy-two-acre tract of land near Bonneville for use as a rustic resort, a place of retreat where visitors might escape the pressures of daily life and find time to revel in God's beauty. He called it Camp Get-A-Way. One of the greatest disappointments of his life occurred when the main lodge burned to the ground in the late 1920s. Unable to rebuild because of financial restraints, the lodge—and the campground—remained silent and unused. Lancaster sold the land to the Oregon State Parks in 1928. The land was passed to the federal government and was used as a service area during construction of Bonneville Dam.

The *Oregonian* praised his "gifts of the spirit, the high enthusiasm, the constant purpose, [and] the fidelity to a fine yet practical idealism."[94] The *Oregon Journal*, his most steadfast supporter over the years, said, "He felt that he was leading a hurrying throng to quiet moments in the temples of nature, where nearness to the Almighty might inspire a worshipful spirit."[95]

Lancaster was never reluctant to share his faith. In a personal letter to Sam Hill in November 1912, he enclosed a typewritten copy of Napoleon's tribute to the Christian religion and encouraged Hill to consider it.

Each weekend during the construction of Bonneville Dam, Lancaster rode the bus out from Portland to observe the progress on the dam and teach in the Sunday school he had built there. In his waning years, he said, "I have built many highways, but the highway from Bonneville Sunday School to Heaven is the best road I ever built."[96]

When Lancaster heard of someone who was homebound, he would visit with his beautiful colored slides and spend an afternoon or evening taking the invalid on a virtual tour of the Columbia River Gorge. His presence and caring were probably the best medicine many of these people received.

He was always ready and anxious to help those who struggled with bodies that would not work—a typewriter for a child who could not hold a pencil, job training for a crippled man.

As the Great Depression took hold of the country and affected the lives of so many, Lancaster shared all he had and then asked for more from those whose circumstances allowed them to share with others. He found jobs for people who needed them, provided food and clothing and encouraged many to seek God's comfort and strength as they continued to press through their difficulties one day at a time.

Before his death, Lancaster received an honorary Master of Arts degree from the University of Oregon.[97]

In 1932, he promoted a new water-level highway. His intent was that the scenic highway might be preserved as a restful place of beauty.

In August 1943, a Liberty Ship was named for him, and a bronze plaque honoring him is displayed beside the front door of Vista House. A Gorge waterfall on Wonder Creek has been given his name. Lancaster Falls is accessed via the Starvation Creek trailhead.

Samuel Christopher Lancaster died on March 4, 1941.

The Columbia River Highway was the brainchild of Sam Hill. It was built by the sweat and elbow grease of common workers and skilled artisans over a period of several years. It was created to lie lightly on the land by the determined efforts of millionaires, news publishers and political activists. Each gave what he had. But Samuel Christopher Lancaster is still considered the heart and soul of the Columbia River Highway. We still call it Lancaster's Road.

THE HIGHWAY TODAY

WHAT IS PAST IS PROLOGUE

By 1954, a water-grade route was completed; it bypassed most of the Columbia River Highway. A few sections of the old highway had been demolished in the process of making the new road. By the late 1950s, sections of this newer highway were being expanded and upgraded to Interstate 80 (now I-84).

In 1966, the freeway was completed and opened to the public. Sections of the Historic Columbia River Highway are still open to vehicle traffic. Where the old road has been demolished or fallen into disrepair, work has been done—and will be done—to restore these sections to their 1920s appearance and open them to the public for nonmotorized recreation. The following is a timeline of the preservation efforts for the road:

- 1971: U.S. Department of the Interior designated Crown Point a National Natural Landmark.
- 1974: Vista House added to the National Register of Historic Places.
- 1979: The Columbia Gorge Hotel added to the National Register of Historic Places.
- 1981: National Park Service completed a comprehensive study of the Columbia River Highway and developed strategies for restoring the highway; Multnomah Falls Lodge, footpath and Benson Bridge placed on the National Register of Historic Places.
- 1983: Fifty-five miles of the extant seventy-four miles of the Columbia River Highway became a National Register of Historic Places–listed linear resource.

- 1984: American Society of Civil Engineers declared the highway a National Historic Civil Engineering Landmark.
- 1985: The View Point Inn placed on the National Register of Historic Places.
- 1986: The Columbia River Gorge National Scenic Area Act (H.R. 5705), signed into law by President Reagan in November, authorized $2.8 million "for the purpose of preparing a program and restoring and reconstructing the Old Columbia River Scenic Highway."
- 1986: Bonneville Dam Historic District established.
- 1987: Senate Bill 766, approved by the sixty-fourth Oregon legislature, established the Historic Columbia River Highway Advisory committee and required the Oregon State Department of Transportation to prepare and manage a historic road program in consultation with the committee.
- 1997: The Historic Columbia River Highway designated a National Scenic Byway, All American Road.
- 2000: Portions of the Columbia River Highway designated as a National Historic Landmark.
- 2002: Abandoned but restored segments of the CRH became a National Recreation Trail.
- As of 2013: Twelve miles of the highway have been reconnected as part of the Historic Columbia River Highway State Trail, with ten more miles of trail remaining to be built.

FRIENDS OF THE HISTORIC COLUMBIA RIVER HIGHWAY

"Just as the builders of the Columbia River Highway celebrated in 1916 the creation of America's first scenic highway, we are joining to restore our road and reconnect it with a series of hiking and biking trails in time for the highway's 100th birthday in 2016."

You can learn more about this organization at www.hcrh.org.

FRIENDS OF THE COLUMBIA GORGE

This group seeks to "vigorously protect the scenic, natural, cultural, and recreational resources of the Columbia River Gorge." You can learn more at www.gorgefriends.org.

Notes

Introduction

1. Lancaster, *Columbia*, 17.
2. Allen, Burns and Sargent, *Cataclysms*, 49–54.
3. Ibid., 43.
4. Allen, *Simon Benson*, 113.
5. Tuhy, *Sam Hill*, 148.

Chapter 1

6. Ibid., 22
7. Ibid.
8. Tuhy's research shows 1865 and also calls into question several of the assertions made by Sam concerning his father. Tuhy suspects lapse of memory and a natural flair for the dramatic rather than outright lying.

Chapter 2

9. Young, e-mail interview.
10. Some sources say typhoid; some say malaria. But malaria is spread by mosquitoes, not contaminated water. Either way, Sam was seriously ill.

11. Marguerite Norris Davis, "The Courage of Samuel Lancaster," appendix A in Lancaster, *Columbia*.
12. Young, e-mail interview.
13. "Life Story," Jackson, TN vertical files, April 29, 1935, 1.
14. The well water contains mineral salts and has a slight electrical charge.

CHAPTER 4

15. Macnab, *Century*, 53.
16. Ibid., 55.
17. Ibid., 51.
18. Ibid., 58.
19. Ibid., 61–62.
20. Ibid., 94.
21. Ibid., 56.
22. Ibid., 94.
23. Ibid., 93.
24. Ibid., 94.
25. Ibid., 86.

CHAPTER 5

26. Allen, *Simon Benson*, 11.
27. Ibid., 15.

CHAPTER 6

28. Peak, "From Immigrant Lad," 16.
29. *Oregon Journal*, November 21, 1920, 5.
30. *Morning Oregonian*, September 29, 1905, 16.

CHAPTER 7

31. U.S. Supreme Court, Omar Spencer, E. Henry Wemme Endowment Fund, 1953.
32. MacColl, *Shaping of a City*.

CHAPTER 10

33. Oswald West, "When We Broke the 'Yaller Hosses,'" in Blakely, *Oswald West*, 12–13.
34. Blakely, *Oswald West*, 16.

CHAPTER 12

35. Allen, *Simon Benson*, 105

CHAPTER 13

36. Tuhy, *Sam Hill*, 140

CHAPTER 14

37. Eva Emery Dye, "Building of Columbia River Highway Greatest Achievement of Kind in Western Hemisphere," *Morning Oregonian*, January 1, 1916.
38. He also reportedly wore out two automobiles and countless tires and paid for all his own gasoline and repairs.
39. Tuhy, *Sam Hill*, 150
40. Samuel Lancaster to Amos Benson, February 7, 1914, "Multnomah County, 1914," Box R RG 76A-90, Oregon State Archives, Salem.
41. Accident report, filed September 10, 1914, Multnomah County Roadmaster's files, Oregon Historical Society.
42. Paul Pintarich, "The Trains Salute When They Go by Fred's Place." *Morning Oregonian*, January 21, 1980. http://www.columbiagorge.org/wp-content/uploads/2013/06/Luscher_Fred_story-interview.pdf.
43. Document releasing Multnomah County from further liability, September 1914, Multnomah County Roadmaster's files, Oregon Historical Society.
44. Antonio De Cicco to Multnomah County Commissioners, July 2, 1914, Multnomah County Roadmaster's files, Oregon Historical Society.
45. Located near the base of Oregon Health Science University's aerial tram.
46. DiBenedetto, interview, June 2007.

CHAPTER 15

47. Elliott, *Report*, 2–3.
48. Ibid., 10.
49. Ibid., 12–13.
50. *Hood River News*, Thursday, January 27, 1966, 2.
51. Lancaster, *Columbia*, 118.
52. Elliott, "Location and Construction," 13.
53. Ibid., 23.
54. Ibid., 17–18.
55. The breakfast was at Margaret Henderson's Crown Point Chalet, which you can read about on pages 136–37.
56. Ibid., 18.

CHAPTER 17

57. Baseline is now called Stark Street.

CHAPTER 18

58. *St. Helens Mist*, Friday, February 19, 1915, 1.
59. Ibid.
60. Ibid.
61. Ibid.
62. Ibid.
63. *Morning Oregonian*, March 6, 1915, 5. The "moral lapses" refer to matters of business integrity.
64. Ibid.
65. *Oregon Journal*, October 1917.
66. Evers, "John Yeon," 86.

CHAPTER 19

67. *Morning Oregonian*, October 25, 1917.
68. Undated news story in the *Portland Telegram*.
69. Beals, interview, September 20, 2006.

70. Walla Walla was a part of the Oregon Territory before Washington became a state.
71. This quote is from a display panel in the Vista House rotunda.

CHAPTER 20

72. *Morning Oregonian*, Sunday, June 29, 1947.

CHAPTER 21

73. Nelson, *Guestbooks*, 13.
74. Ibid., 14.
75. Ibid., passim.
76. Allen, *Simon Benson*, 130.

CHAPTER 22

77. Multnomah County Roadmaster's files, Oregon Historical Society.
78. Ibid.
79. *Oregon Journal*, June 19, 1918.
80. See more about this on page 166.
81. R.H. Baldock to *Oregonian*, published in *Oregonian*, December 8, 1954, 26.
82. *Hood River News*, "OSU Engineers Use New Material to Shore Up Old Bridge in Gorge," Saturday, October 17, 1998, A6.

CHAPTER 23

83. Letter from the files at Maryhill Museum of Art.
84. Bowlby, "Columbia Highway," 18.
85. Allen, *Simon Benson*, 134.
86. Ibid.
87. Ibid.
88. Tuhy, *Sam Hill*, 129.
89. *Sunday Oregonian*, June 27, 1915.

90. Klickitat is the county in Washington State where Maryhill is located. Stonehenge is about four miles east of the museum.

91. Fred Lockley quoted in the *Oregon Journal*, January 19, 1930.

92. Lancaster also wrote *Romance of the Gateway: Through the Cascade Range* and *History and Legends of the Columbia*.

93. Lancaster, *Columbia*, preface.

94. Fahl, "S.C. Lancaster," 132.

95. Ibid.

96. *Sunday Oregonian*, "Sam Lancaster Put Beauty in NW," July 11, 1965, 8.

97. Ibid., July 7, 1963, 38.

BIBLIOGRAPHY

BOOKS

Allen, Alice Benson. *Simon Benson: Northwest Lumber King.* Portland: OR: Binfords & Mort, 1971.

Allen, John Eliot, and Marjorie Burns, with Sam C. Sargent. *Cataclysms on the Columbia.* Portland, OR: Timber Press, 1986.

Allen, John Eliot. *The Magnificent Gateway.* Forest Grove, OR: Timber Press, 1979.

Alt, David. *Glacial Lake Missoula and Its Humongous Floods.* Missoula, MT: Mountain Press Publishing Company, 2001.

Blakely, Joe R. *Oswald West.* Eugene, OR: Crane Dance Publications, 2012.

Bullard, Oral. *Lancaster's Road: The Historic Columbia River Scenic Highway.* Beaverton, OR: TMS Book Service, 1982.

Hadlow, Robert W. *Elegant Arches, Soaring Spans.* Corvallis: Oregon State University Press, 2001.

Harrison, John A. *A Woman Alone: Mona Bell, Sam Hill and the Mansion on Bonneville Rock.* Portland, OR: Frank Amato Publications Inc., 2009.

Kloos, Jeanette B. *Historic Columbia River Highway Master Plan.* Salem: Oregon Department of Transportation, 2006.

Lancaster, Samuel C. *The Columbia: America's Great Highway through the Cascade Mountains to the Sea.* Atglen, PA: Schiffer Publishing Ltd., 2004.

————. *Romance of the Gateway.* Portland, OR: J.K. Gill, n.d. First published 1929 by Press of Kilham Stationery and Printing Company.

MacColl, E. Kimbark. *The Shaping of a City: Business and Politics in Portland, Oregon, 1885 to 1915.* Portland, OR: Georgian Press Company, 1976.

Macnab, Gordon. *A Century of News and People in the* East Oregonian *1875–1975.* Pendleton, OR: East Oregonian Publishing Co., 1975.

Mershon, Clarence E. *The Columbia River Highway: From the Sea to the Wheat Fields of Eastern Oregon.* Portland, OR: Guardian Peaks Enterprises, 2006.

————. *East of the Sandy: The Columbia River Highway.* Portland, OR: Guardian Peaks Inc., 2001.

Nelson, Clifford D. *The Guestbooks of Crown Point Chalet (1915–1927).* Self-published, 2001.

Plotts, Lois Davis. *Maryhill Sam Hill and Me.* Camas, WA: Post Publications Inc., 1978.

Ravenel, Samuel W., CE. *Ravenel's Road Primer for School Children.* Chicago: A.C. McClurg & Co., 1912.

Salt, Harriet. *Mighty Engineering Feats.* Philadelphia: Penn Publishing Company, 1937.

Scharlach, Bernice. *Big Alma: San Francisco's Alma Spreckles.* San Francisco, CA: Scottwall Associates, Publishers, 1990.

Smith, Dwight A., James B. Norman and Pieter T. Dykman. *Historic Highway Bridges of Oregon.* Salem: Oregon Department of Transportation, 1985.

Stewart, Anita. *A Taste of Comfort.* Portland, OR: C&D Publishing, 1993.

Tuhy, John E. *Sam Hill: The Prince of Castle Nowhere.* Portland, OR: Timber Press, 1983.

Wade, Elisabeth Ehrens. *Samuel Hill from Samuel Hill.* Prescott, AZ: Classic Press, 1986.

PERSONAL INTERVIEWS

Beals, Marion Ackerman, daughter of Frank Ackerman. Interview with the author, several occasions between 2006 and 2008.

DiBenedetto, (Americo) Benny, Portland architect. Interview with the author, June 2007.

Young, Ellnora Lancaster Rose. E-mail interview with the author, several occasions between 2006 and 2013.

PAPERS

Assorted papers from files at Maryhill Museum of Art.

Benson, S., W.L. Thompson, R.A. Booth and Herbert Nunn. *Third Biennial Report of the Oregon State Highway Commission.* Salem: Oregon State Highway Commission, State Printing Department, 1919.

Elliott, John Arthur. "The Location and Construction of the Mitchell Point Section of the Columbia River Highway, Oregon." Thesis submitted for the degree of Civil Engineer, University of Washington, 1929.

———. *Report on Columbia Highway Hood River Co. 1914.* Oregon Department of Transportation.

Evers, Michael J. "John Yeon and the Construction of the Columbia River Highway." Thesis, San Diego State University, 1992.

Hadlow, Robert W. National Historic Landmark Nomination. U.S. Department of the Interior, National Park Service.

Hadlow, Robert W., PhD, and Amanda Joy Pietz. Historic Columbia River Highway Oral History Final Report SR 500-261.

Historic American Engineering Record (HAER). Historic Columbia River Highway, Crown Point Viaduct. No. OR-36-C.

Krier, Patricia Connolly. "Toward a Civilized Wilderness: Samuel Hill's Contribution to Pacific Northwest Highways, 1899–1916." Master's thesis, University of Oregon, June 1984.

Lancaster, Samuel. "Practical Road Building in Madison County, Tennessee." *Yearbook of the Department of Agriculture.* U.S. government, 1905.

"Multnomah County, 1914." Box R RG 76A-90, Oregon State Archives, Salem.

U.S. Supreme Court Records and Briefs, 1832–1978. Omar Spencer. E. Henry Wemme Endowment Fund, 1953.

MAGAZINE ARTICLES

Bowlby, Henry L. "The Columbia Highway in Oregon." *American Forestry* (August 1916): 12–22.

Fahl, Ronald J. "S.C. Lancaster and the Columbia River Highway: Engineer as Conservationist." *Oregon Historical Quarterly* 74: 101–44.

Good Roads magazine, many issues, available at Washington State University in Pullman, WA.

BIBLIOGRAPHY

Howard, Randall R. "Through the Columbia River Gorge by Auto." *Oregon Digital*: 303.

Hughson, Oliver Greeley. "When We Logged the Columbia" *Oregon Historical Quarterly* 60: 189–91.

"Interesting Westerners." *Sunset* (May 1925): 28–29.

"Life Story of Sam C. Lancaster, Former City Engineer, Inspiring." News article from Jackson, TN vertical files, April 29, 1935, 1.

Peak, Mayme Ober. "From Immigrant Lad to Empire Builder: The Poor French Canadian Boy Who Built the Columbia River Highway." *Sunset* (June 1926): 16–18, 62.

Sell, David J. "Roll On Columbia!" *American Road* 3, no. 3 (Autumn 2005).

"Tunnel Creator Honored by Scholarship." *(University of Washington) Columns* (March 2002).

Warren, George C. "Drain! Drain!! And Drain Some More!!!" *Good Roads* (August 5, 1916).

NEWSPAPERS

Gresham Outlook, Gresham, Oregon.

Hood River News, Hood River, Oregon.

Morning Oregonian, Portland, Oregon.

Oregon Journal, Portland, Oregon.

Portland Telegram, Portland, Oregon.

St. Helens Mist, St. Helens, Oregon.

Sunday Oregonian, Portland, Oregon.

OTHER

Friends of the Historic Columbia River Highway and Historic Columbia River Highway Advisory Committee. *The Historic Columbia River Highway: World Class Adventure from Portland to The Dalles, Reconnecting the Historic Highway as a Trail.* Booklet published by the Friends of the Historic Columbia River Highway and the Historic Columbia River Highway Advisory Committee, March 2009.

Multnomah County Roadmaster's Files, located at Oregon Historical Society Research Library.

INDEX

About the Author

Peg Willis, a lifelong resident of the Pacific Northwest, grew up loving the Columbia River Highway. More than just a way to get from one place to another, it was a playground and an adventure. Since retirement from teaching, Peg has pursued a longtime dream of becoming more intimately acquainted with this historic beauty, its origins and its secrets. Her search has led her to volunteer with the Vista House and the Friends of the Historic Columbia River Highway. Her work has been published in a number of magazines and regional newspapers. Peg and her husband, Jim, have three amazing sons, three perfect daughters-in-law and seven awesome grandchildren—all of whom also live in Oregon.

CPSIA information can be obtained
at www.ICGtesting.com
Printed in the USA
LVHW051033130122
708377LV00012B/576